BEHIND THE
FASHIONABLE
DRAPES

THE FOUNDATION BEHIND FASHION: ART, SCIENCE, AND RIGOROUS STANDARDS OF PRODUCT DEVELOPMENT

PARVEZ AHMED PESHIMAM

ISBN
Paperback 979-8-89632-303-7
Hardcase 979-8-89699-367-4

CONTENTS

Contents

PREFACE

In "Behind The Fashionable Drapes," Parvez Ahmed Peshimam unfolds a narrative that beckons readers into the alluring realm of fashion, guided by his seasoned expertise amassed over three decades in the industry. With a meticulous eye for detail and a passion for storytelling, Peshimam crafts an immersive journey that transcends the mere glamour of haute couture, delving deep into the intricate processes that define the creation of every collection and season.

From the initial spark of inspiration to the dazzling debut on the runway, Peshimam meticulously traces the evolution of fashion, offering readers a behind-the-scenes glimpse into the labyrinthine workings of the industry. Through vivid prose and insightful anecdotes, he demystifies the complex web of departments, teams, and collaborations that converge to bring designer visions to life. Each chapter unfolds like a carefully tailored garment, revealing the symbiotic dance between creativity and craftsmanship that defines modern fashion.

What sets "Behind The Fashionable Drapes" apart is its intimate portrayal of the human endeavor behind each stitch and seam. Peshimam not only celebrates the artistry of designers but also shines a spotlight on the intricate craftsmanship poured in by the unsung heroes—the pattern makers, artisans, and technicians—who labor tirelessly to transform concepts into reality. His narrative is as much a tribute to their skill and dedication as it is a testament to the industry's relentless pursuit of innovation.

For fashion enthusiasts, the book offers a treasure trove of insights and revelations, providing a deeper understanding of the meticulous planning and execution that underpin each fashion cycle. Entrepreneurs will find invaluable lessons in Peshimam's exploration of business strategies and creative processes, gleaned from his rich tapestry of experiences.

Through eloquent writing and profound observations, "Behind The Fashionable Drapes" transcends its subject matter, becoming a compelling exploration of human creativity and collaboration. Peshimam's narrative prowess transforms each page into a canvas where dreams are woven into silk and satin, urging readers to appreciate the artistry and dedication that shape global fashion trends. This book is more than a chronicle of style; it is a testament to the transformative power of passion and perseverance in an industry where innovation meets imagination.

CHAPTER 1

SHIMMERING ELEGANCE –
THE GLAMOUR IN FASHION

THE RUNWAY CASES

Runway shows are the ultimate platform for brands and fashion designers to show their creativity. Every show is carefully curated to align with the designer's vision. From setting the stage, the lights, the music, and every element is a piece of the designer's narrative unfolding on the runway. These shows set the tone for upcoming trends and styles. While top designers unveil their latest collections, presenting a preview of what is coming in the world of fashion; similarly, influential fashion editors, buyers, and industry experts closely scrutinize these collections to identify emerging trends and to determine which creation will resonate with consumer choices. These avant-garde displays conflate fashion and art, making every show an unforgettable spectacle.

Attending a high-profile fashion show is considered a mammoth honor in the fashion industry. Invitations are often limited to industry icons, VIPs, and persuasive members of the press. Securing an invitation at a prestigious show is evidence to one's status and influence in the fashion arena. From prominent movie stars to music icons and sports stars, celebrities are invited to grace the front-row seats to witness the latest designs firsthand. Their presence adds an extra layer of excitement and media attention to the event.

High-profile fashion shows garner extensive media coverage from all over the world. While mainstream media agencies report highlights of the event, real-time updates and commentary are provided by fashion journalists, photographers, and bloggers flooding the social media. The impact of these shows reaches far beyond the runway, influencing fashion discourse and consumer behavior globally. These events are used by designers and brands to draw customers, establish connections with retailers, and create a buzz about their products. In the cutthroat world of fashion, publicity from a well-executed runway show may result in more sales and greater brand recognition.

Red carpet events are the height of elegance in the entertainment business, where stars wow the globe with their exquisite style and daring fashion choices. Whether it's the Oscars, the Met Gala, or the Cannes Film Festival, these legendary occasions provide a stage for celebrities to steal the show and for designers to showcase their works.

THE POWER OF CELEBRITY ENDORSEMENT

Lupita Nyong'o's performance at the 2014 Academy Awards is an amazing example. How the actress swiftly climbed to the top of best-dressed rankings and cemented her place as a fashion legend with her breathtaking pale blue Prada gown embellished with over 6,000 pearls. Nyong'o's selection not only demonstrated her great taste but also honored originality and diversity in the fashion industry, it served as an inspiration to a multitude of designers and fashion devotees worldwide.

Similarly, Rihanna's presence at the 2015 Met Gala is another iconic red-carpet event that made an impact. The event's theme was "China: Through the Looking Glass," and Rihanna made an impression in a stunning yellow Guo Pei gown featuring an intricate train that extended several feet. The intricate design of the dress along with Rihanna's self-assured style perfectly encapsulated the subject, inspiring admiration and amazement on social media. Her audacious decision pushed boundaries and defied conventions while simultaneously paying tribute to Chinese culture and reinventing red carpet style.

Celebrity endorsements have the capacity to significantly influence fashion trends and increase brand awareness to previously unheard-of levels. Celebrities are powerful tastemakers who not only promote designer goods but also give them an air of exclusivity and desirability through their connections on social media.

Jennifer Lawrence's stunning Dior gown at the 2013 Academy Awards which cemented her place in fashion history and propelled Dior to prominence as one of the most sought-after luxury fashion businesses. In a similar vein, Brad Pitt's 2020 Golden Globes suit, designed by Brioni enhanced the brand's recognition for classic style and exquisite tailoring among both customers and fashion journalists.

Social media has developed into a potent platform for celebrity endorsements in addition to red carpet appearances, giving marketers the opportunity to interact directly with customers and reach a larger audience. Adidas's collaboration with Kylie Jenner is the finest illustration. Through her Instagram account, the reality TV star turned beauty mogul regularly posts pictures and videos of herself wearing Adidas athleisure clothing, effectively using her large following to promote the brand's goods and way of life. As a result of Jenner's support, Adidas has experienced a notable increase in visibility and sales.

Celebrity endorsements has the power to break beyond conventional barriers and influence public discourse. During her royal tour in South Africa, Meghan Markle wore a modest white blouse from the sustainable fashion brand Everlane, which caused a global uproar and raised awareness of ethical and sustainable fashion practices. In addition to increasing Everlane's sales, Markle's support brought attention to the significance of responsible consumerism in the fashion industry.

FASHION ENTERTAINMENT

Fashion magazines, such as Vogue, Elle, and Harper's Bazaar, are the height of elegance and luxury in the business. These magazines have a significant impact on how fashion is portrayed, how people choose to dress, and how designers, photographers, stylists, and models are celebrated for their artistic abilities.

Photographers are the masterminds behind the camera, using their distinct viewpoints and creative vision to capture the spirit of the editorial idea. Stylists are essential in converting the designer's vision into aesthetically pleasing ensembles that appeal to the intended audience. Models are the living embodiment of the editorial story; they give life to the designer's works and draw readers with awe with their grace, expressiveness, and charm.

The collaboration of these artistic energies produces fashion editorials that are more than just visually appealing; they provide an insight into how fashion and culture are always changing. Fashion magazines encourage readers to discover new avenues for style and self-expression by pushing the limits of creativity and challenging conventional conventions with their avant-garde imagery, bold aesthetics, and creative notions.

While glossy magazines and fashion editorials are essential for creating the cultural zeitgeist, influencing fashion trends, and advancing the level of fashion artistry. Viewers can also get an engrossing peek into the inner workings of the fashion business through documentaries and films, which offer insights into the drama, glamour, and inventiveness that, characterize this dynamic world. These documentaries and films illuminate the artistry, craftsmanship, and cultural significance of fashion, offering anything from behind-the-scenes glimpses at the creation of classic fashion publications to dramatized descriptions of the lives of fashion insiders.

Some of the following are a good watch and informative for fashion enthusiasts. I make it a point to recommend my team to watch these at their leisure for insights into the fashion industry.

"The September Issue" (2009), directed by R.J. Cutler, provides a close-up and insightful look into the production of Vogue magazine's September 2007 edition, which is recognized as the year's most significant issue. The film follows Anna Wintour, the legendary editor-in-chief of Vogue, and her group of editors, photographers, and stylists as they make their way through the competitive world of fashion publishing.

"Dior and I" (2014), under the direction of Frédéric Tcheng, provides an intimate glimpse into the creation of Raf Simons' first couture collection as the House of Dior's creative director. The documentary chronicles the relentless efforts of Simons and his team, from the first sketches to the last runway show, as they strive to realize his vision.

"Bill Cunningham New York" (2010) honors the late Bill Cunningham, a renowned street-style photographer who captured New York City's fashion scene for more than 50 years, in this Richard Press-directed film. The documentary provides an insight into Cunningham's life and career, tracing his rise from modest millinery origins to his legendary stature as a cultural and fashion icon.

"The Devil Wears Prada" (2006) is based on Lauren Weisberger's novel. It provides a satirical look at the competitive world of fashion publishing and the sacrifices one must make to succeed in the business. Starring Meryl Streep and Anne Hathaway, the film is directed by David Frankel and tells the fictional story of a young, ambitious journalist who gets hired as Miranda Priestly's assistant.

"McQueen" is a documentary on visionary fashion designer Alexander McQueen, directed by Ian Bonhôte and Peter Ettedgui. The documentary delves into the designer's creative genius, his struggles with fame and addiction, and his lasting impact on the fashion business through historical footage, interviews with friends, family, and coworkers, and footage of McQueen's famed catwalk shows.

These are just a few of the fascinating fashion documentaries and films that help audiences understand the craftsmanship, ingenuity, and cultural significance of the fashion industry. These documentaries and films celebrate the rich heritage of fashion and its profound impact on our lives and culture, whether they take a behind-the-scenes look at the development of iconic fashion magazines or delve into the lives and careers of great designers.

GLOBAL FASHION ICONS AND INFLUENCERS

Global fashion heroes and influencers have had a lasting impact on the industry, driving trends, defining aesthetics, and inspiring generations with their ingenuity, inventiveness, and unique sense of style. From renowned designers who changed the way we dressed to modern-day tastemakers who dominate social media platforms, these powerful personalities have broken down barriers, reinvented beauty standards, and secured their standing as cultural icons.

Gabrielle "Coco" Chanel, is widely acknowledged as one of the most influential figures in fashion history." It is undoubtedly true as she transformed women's fashion with timeless designs that prioritized comfort, elegance, and simplicity. Chanel's revolutionary design approach liberated women from the restrictions of corsets, which were widely used then, ushering in a new era of modernity and sophistication with the classic Chanel suit and the little black dress.

Gianni Versace, another visionary designer known for his strong use of color, audacious prints, and sumptuous creations, embodied the excess and glamour of the 1980s and 1990s. Versace reinvented luxury fashion with his provocative pieces and celebrity-studded runway presentations, leaving an enduring imprint on the industry.

Yohji Yamamoto is a prominent Japanese fashion designer known for his avant-garde designs and deconstructed forms. His work has had a significant impact on the worldwide fashion landscape. Yamamoto's minimalist design and emphasis on craftsmanship have reinvented concepts of beauty and elegance, winning him global respect and admiration.

Anna Wintour, editor-in-chief of Vogue magazine, has wielded unrivaled influence in the fashion world, defining trends, recognizing talent, and advocating for diversity and inclusion. With her characteristic bob hairdo and huge sunglasses, Wintour is not just a fashion star, but also a formidable force in the media landscape, directing fashion journalism and setting the agenda for the industry as a whole.

Alexander McQueen was a visionary designer known for his avant-garde designs, spectacular runway displays, and darkly romantic style. His creations pushed the limits of art and fashion. McQueen charmed spectators with his precise craftsmanship and unrestrained originality, leaving a lasting legacy that inspires designers and fashion fans to this day.

Karl Lagerfeld, Chanel's creative director for almost three decades, was a larger-than-life personality in the fashion world. His trademark white ponytail, black sunglasses, and razor-sharp humor cannot be missed. Lagerfeld, was a master of reinvention, continually pushing the frontiers of fashion while also embracing new technologies and trends.

Gigi and Bella Hadid, are the two of the most famous faces in the modeling world, they have become style icons in their own right, appearing on the covers of numerous publications, walking the runway for leading designers, and collaborating with fashion firms on lucrative campaigns. The Hadid sisters' flawless beauty, immaculate style, and large social media following have made them synonymous with modern-day glamor and refinement.

On the Indian front, Manish Malhotra is a leading Indian fashion designer celebrated for his work in Bollywood. His influence extends beyond fashion, as he has also styled numerous iconic looks for films, earning accolades and widespread acclaim.

Sabyasachi Mukherjee is a distinguished Indian designer known for his exquisite bridal wear and revival of traditional crafts. His label, by his name, is synonymous with luxury and elegance, making him a sought-after name for brides and fashion enthusiasts worldwide.

A pioneer in Indian fashion, Ritu Kumar has been instrumental in promoting traditional Indian textiles and craftsmanship. With decades of experience, she has played a crucial role in shaping Indian fashion, earning numerous honors for her contributions.

All these figures have made profound contributions to the world of fashion, earning them widespread recognition within the fashion community. Each icon possesses a distinct style, a unique way of presenting themselves that exudes grace and sophistication. However, our attention will now shift from the individuals to the attire that adorns them.

SNEAK PEEK

The birth of every fashion article is a unique journey. Each piece of clothing carries a story, woven from its inception to its realization. Whether driven by a desire to fulfill a need, bridge a gap, or satisfy a craving, the designer's intent shapes this journey. It typically begins with a simple sketch, a raw idea on paper. From there, it progresses through meticulous stages of product development—where fabrics are chosen, patterns refined, and details perfected—before finally reaching its ultimate owner.

This process is more than just a series of steps; it's a creative evolution. Each stage is crucial in transforming an initial concept into a tangible, wearable piece of art. The result is not just clothing, but a statement—a reflection of the designer's vision and the wearer's identity. In the end, the attire not only enhances the individual but also embodies the intricate and thoughtful process that brought it to life.

Let's raise the curtains and embark on a journey of exploration, visiting every step in the process of creating a fashion clothing item from start to finish. We'll pause at key stages to understand the mechanisms and tasks of each department that adds value to the initial sketch, shaping it into the work of art envisioned by the designer.

CHAPTER 2

SKETCH TO STITCHES – DESIGN INITIATION

EXPLORATION OF DESIGN

Inspiration could come from anything, it could be a drawing on a billboard, a leaf in a garden or at the side of a street, from a motif embroidered on a bystander's jacket in a caffe. A creative mind ignites when it is triggered by absorbing matter through any of their senses. Designers explore these senses to envision how they want to nurture their creativity and develop their designs.

Current events could also ignite creativity. Designers may capture information from social media or the news that inspires them to do something new and unique. It could be some kind of a demonstration, a fad or a trend or even a dancing twist or a move. Designers would use these aspects to create their designs that reflect the current situation and their feelings about them.

Designers put together a set of mood boards consisting of images, textile swatches, accessories, trinkets and anything that could inspire them. The creation of mood boards aid in visualizing a set of ideas, styles, colors, textures, accessories and trims that would eventually shape the collections. Mood boards act as a communication tool providing a visual summary of the intended outcomes. By piecing everything together with each component necessary to complete the picture, they aim to create something unique that they can proudly share with the world.

INITIAL SKETCHES

Sketching is one of the important activities in the early stages in the creative process for a fashion designer. It is the stage when imagination takes shape on paper. Designers convert their imaginations into forms to explore, fine-tune and eventually communicate their concepts to the wider circle of colleagues.

Designers equip themselves with sketchpads, digital tablets, etc. to start on a blank board. Armed with a pencil or a stylus they begin their journey of experimentation with lines, shapes, and proportions. This early phase is like experiencing freedom by opening windows allowing ideas to flow unobstructed.

The entire idea of sketching is to generate silhouettes for the intended collection or group of styles. Silhouette is an outline of a garment, a shape that the fabric is transformed to fit or drape a body. It is important to visualize the aesthetic appeal of a garment along with its comfort and utility. The studios would be buzzing with activity as the designers experiment with various silhouettes from snugged fitting to free-flowing, structured vs. unstructured styles. Eventually, they will settle with the one that best suits their vision.

It is crucial to include details such as shape of pockets, collars, darts, and seam structure for constructing the garments. Every detail, no matter how minor is important to be communicated and defined on the sketch for crystal clear communication with other departments.

During the sketching process, designers need to take into account the techniques and complexities of garment production. It is important to consider the process of pattern making, drafting and cutting, along with the functions of the assembly line. This is to ensure their ideas are not only aesthetically appealing but also practical to be carried out in production. This requires a necessary understanding of garment construction to skillfully convert 2D artworks into 3D reality. The technical designers or garment technicians add informative elements to the flat sketches to transform them into visually striking masterpieces as you will read in the "Apparel Engineering" chapter number 3.

FABRIC AND COLOR SELECTION

The selection of fabrics is a key component of the apparel design process. The right fabric can convey the intended message of a collection with the overall appearance.

Designers diligently examine the fabric texture, weight, and drape to ensure that their products accurately align with their vision.

The designers start by acknowledging which qualities the garment requires to acquire. Since fabrics come is various qualities from smooth as silk to rough and textured, it is significant to anticipate how the quality of the fabric will complement the wearer's physical experience. For example, a designer aiming for a refined elegant style may opt for silk or satin while a designer targeting a bohemian look might choose to go with linen or cotton with a crude texture.

The fabric weight plays a crucial role in influencing the volume and structure of the garments as it impacts how they fit and drape on the body. As chiffon is a lightweight fabric it is good for flowing and delicate designs and heavy-weight fabrics such as wool and denim offer warmth and structure making it a good choice for winter wear and outerwear.

While the choice of fabric textures, quality and weight are important, the choice of color plays an important role in setting the intended mood of a collection. To make sure the selected colors appeal to their targeted audience, designers take into account trends, the psychology of color, cultural significance, and forecasting into account before choosing a color theme. Colors have the power to evoke feelings and establish connections, hence designers make the most of this element to create chronicles through their creation.

Colors in cool tones of blues and greens induce serenity and tranquility, while warm tones of oranges and reds are tilted towards passion and power. Designers experiment and play to strike a visually contrasting balance to trigger specific feelings for their styles.

TEXTILE AND PRINT DESIGNS

The development teams as far as I have experienced have always been fascinated with the opportunity to play with colors and prints. They love visiting factories to gain hands-on experience when developing prints and choosing colors. They are mesmerized every time they witness the efforts that goes into striking the right balance with the prints, colors and the base fabric. While some colors may appear striking and aesthetic on some fabrics, the same colors may look dull and pale on some other fabrics. This needs to be especially considered in collections which are made up of multiple fabrics.

The color chemists working with the colors in the dyeing and printing factories are quite skillful in identifying these limitations and differences in fabric compositions. Many a times several options are made for solid colors called lab-dips and the same options created for prints are called strike-offs based on the specified

Pantone numbers. Pantones are color specifications which a major part of the fashion industry globally uses to communicate color standards. The multiple options of lab-dips and strike-offs generated may have a minor or negligible difference. But these differences sometimes help to coordinate with the other elements of the garments by viewing the bigger picture holistically.

Color submissions are evaluated for color specifications using a spectrophotometer for electronic reading or using a grey gradient scale for manual evaluations.

A spectrophotometer is a scientific instrument used to measure the intensity of light at different wavelengths. It works by passing light through a sample and measuring the amount of light that is absorbed, transmitted, or reflected by the sample at each wavelength. This measurement allows for the analysis of the sample's color, concentration, or chemical composition, depending on the application.

In practical terms, a spectrophotometer is used to create a spectrum, which is a graph that shows how the intensity of light varies with wavelength. The resulting data provides detailed information about the optical properties of the sample. This makes the spectrophotometer a versatile tool in many fields, including chemistry, biology, physics, material science and of course the fashion industry.

I have always found the manual color evaluation process to be far more accurate as compared to the reading generated by a spectrophotometer. Especially when a garment has multiple fabrics and a combination of dye and prints on different parts of the garment in different fabrications, the evaluation is more precise when seen in the form of a garment on either a live body or a mannequin. The fall and drape of the fabrics, the reflection of light from the fabric surface, and the flow and movement of the garment when in motion displays optimal color matching and compatibility among other garments in the collection and with the different parts of the same garment. The color matching in textile when the colors are being developed and the color matching and evaluation procedure is a slightly tricky activity. This technique helps in analyzing and calibrating colors by providing a reference point to judge color accuracy, consistency, and variations.

Making mistakes is a natural part of the process. The professional color chemists with amazing technical abilities gained over many years of experience have mastered the art of color mixing and the color formulations so that the print or dye although done on different fabrics in different compositions, will collectively sit together satisfactorily as a collection.

Interactive and seamless communication between the teams is vital for the success of any project. Any decision to make on changes in the colors must be mutually agreed between the first-tier collaborators for the sake of clarity. We will discuss more on the first and second tier teams towards the end of this chapter.

FORMING COLLECTIONS

At the point when the designers have decided on the 3 major elements that is fabrics, prints/ colors and silhouettes, they move on to creating collections. Collections are a set of styles gathered with common elements to form a story. The connecting factor could be prints, colors or shapes. A range of strategies are formed to make sure the collections have the right balance between statement styles, best sellers and transitional styles. The ratio of distribution for the best sellers is the highest with smaller quantities allotted to the other two groups.

Statement styles are those where the designers are unleashed to explore new fashion trends or create a unique product that has never been done before. These are experimental as it may be a hit, or a miss and the business is confident about taking this risk. Best sellers are items that are basic and styles that have been successful in the past and the business needs to repeat them with slight modifications as they have proven to be commercially safe.

The transitional styles are a combination of the best sellers with elements from the statement styles. These styles help to bridge the gap between the best sellers and statement styles. The transitional styles bring together elements from both extremes merging wearability with innovation.

Every business has their own strategy when forming ratios for the 3 primary buckets. There is no set formula, it is at the discretion of a company to choose what has worked best for them in the past. They may refer to the merchandising planners' sales and forecast reports to reach a conclusion, while adapting best industry practices they have observed from the markets in the regions of their retail operations.

Designers experiment with proportions to generate unified styles to cover across dimensions and structures from well-fitted formalwear and sportswear to loose-fit flowing casual dresses and pants to oversized casual and street wear. Designers form collections that combine basic essentials, statement items, and transitional silhouettes to create captivating narratives. Collections will often reflect the signature of the designer through their personal touch and creative vision.

THE PRESENTATION

As the designers are experimenting with different fabrics, styles, prints and silhouettes to share their seasons vison with the team, things aren't always easy as we would like it to be. Most often than not plans do not go as intended, which then requires improvisation. Perhaps a certain fabric or a component does not go well with the design, or the final outcome may not be compatible with the original vision. Difficult choices need to me made in these situations considering that these minute variations may have a deep impact on the results. In times like these designers need to swiftly act on dropping the unsuitable element that isn't functioning or change it with an alternate element that fits the concept better.

Adapting to constant changes and improvising is part of the creative process. A mature team of designers not only welcome the challenges of change but also adapt themselves to an opportunity of making something better. They understand that every chance and iteration take them closer to their final objective. The team goes through the minor and major details as they prepare to unveil the season's preliminary creations.

The selection of elements carefully chosen by the designers during the conceptual stages through the mood boards is at the heart of this presentation. The design team initiates the presentation by going through the overview of the seasons concept, followed by the work of each designer in conjunction with the respective categories the collections relate to. Each style, fabric, print, colors, accessories, and decoration are thoroughly examined to ensure they blend with the desired look perfectly.

As the designers present their respective creations, feedback is given by the management comprising of the retail and merchandising planning managers. The presence of retail managers and sales team who are the first contact with consumers is to ensure the proposed designs are aligned with their expectations. And the presence of the merchandising planning team is to ensure the proposed styles have the ability to generate like-to-like sales compared to the same duration or same season of last year.

With the presentation and collecting important feedback brings us close to the initial launch of the season's preparation from the design team. It is now time to bring on the other expertise on board to begin phase two of the product development process. Up until this moment the designers are working within the confinements of their team and department. Starting now on it is more of a collaborative working mechanism which requires flawless interdepartmental coordination. The common key factor for the success of all teams irrespective of their activity is communication.

COMMUNICATION

The "Product Development" process in the fashion industry is highly dynamic. A design may start as a particular silhouette in a respective fabric in a certain print or colors, but certain aspects of the design may change as the item advances on the product development route due to various justified modifications the team thinks is necessary for the success of the style. These changes happen throughout the various stages of the product development cycle.

The network of dialogues that connect departments and the flow of ideas as they are developed are imperative to be shared with the wider teams.

A majority of the corporates I have had the privilege of working in or collaborating with have separate departments or teams of designers, garment technicians, purchase departments, apparel merchandizers/ planners, quality assurance, logistics, visual merchandizing, marketing and retail teams. I place these departments as first-tier teams. These first-tier teams are directly related to the products and any slight changes in dimensions on product specifications impact most departments if not all.

The second-tier teams like finance, legal, human resources, information technology, social and corporate responsibility, together with learning and development though not directly linked to the product but may have minor implications dealing with the dynamics of product development cycle. And in my opinion, it is good practice to keep them in the loop for awareness.

These teams have weekly interdepartmental meetings where they share and exchange ideas and progress to advancing stages. Everything discussed in a particular week will be worked upon and shared in the next weekly meeting. This process creates a gap of 5 working days between each information exchange. This is an area where we need change to accommodate frequent exchange of ideas and quick responses to points discussed in interdepartmental meetings to competitively stay on the critical path of product development. This is where I again emphasize on the importance of communication for successful collaboration between individuals and teams.

However, there is no magic solution, what works for one company may not work for another. Creative Management of the companies must decide what are the best industry practices that will suit their process of product development interdepartmentally.

CHAPTER 3

APPAREL ENGINEERING – CRAFTING SPECIFICATIONS

DECODING DESIGN BRIEFS

Picking up from the design presentation which marks completion of the first phase of product development we move on to breaking down information into digestible chunks. By this stage the team would be clear of the designs that are confirmed to advance to the next stages while the remaining few may require restyling. The confirmed styles are now required to be sent to the sampling team of the manufacturer to transform into garments, which are labeled as "First Samples". For the manufacturing team to interpret the designs could lead to many stages of sampling and resampling, therefore a mediator is required to decode the designs into smaller chunks of information for the sampling team to understand and execute. The mediators in this case are "Technologists" or "Garment Technicians".

The technical team could be part of the design team, an extension of the design team or a completely separate identity. It is at the discretion of the company management based on past experiences what works best for the smooth functioning of the many teams involved in the product development process. Irrespective of where they sit in the hierarchy, the primary function of the technologists is to decode the designs and add additional information with technical specifications. The objective is to prepare "Technical Specification Packs" (tech-packs) for the sampling teams ease of understanding in generating a sample.

This process involves providing specifications such as a measurement chart to help the pattern masters of the sampling team to generate 2D patterns into 3D apparel. It involves giving guidelines on the use of the right quality of fabric for the style, along with specific fabric count, construction with weight and composition. Communicate colors through the universal standard of pantone color numbers. Provide print specification in terms of direction and dimensions. To specify placement of pockets, dimensions of pockets, positioning of seams, kind of seam, stitches required per inch, button placement, size of buttons and buttonholes, specification of fasteners, collar shapes and finishing techniques. It is also essential to provide guidelines on packing specifications.

All this information is part of the technical specifications which help the manufacturer to gather the raw materials and prepare the requested sample. It also helps to ascertain the costs involved to be able to calculate and present a competitive quote. Providing the above information in the simplest manner by the technologists and receiving the information by the sampling team in the same specification and understanding is vital for the successful creation of the first sample to achieve highest accuracy rate.

THE SAMPLING CHAMPIONS

Upon receiving the technical specification packs from the design house, the manufacturer's sampling team is required to study and confirm their understanding of the provided guidelines. The sampling team is free to coordinate with the technologists in case any point needs to be clarified. Once the doubts are clarified, the sampling team swings into action on 2 fronts, pattern making and sourcing.

The pattern master will start to generate a pattern based on the provided measurement charts and technical guidelines. Patterns for all the silhouettes are generated either manually or with the aid of a digitizer. While the manual method may take hours the digitizer can draft a pattern in a very short time upon entering the measurements of specific dimensions. Almost all factories are now equipped with computer aided machinery to slash the turnaround time, improve efficiency and precision.

Upon mastering the base size accurately, the patterns are graded across other sizes to generate a size set. In almost every brand the base is a size "M" (medium) unless specified otherwise. Keeping size M as the base the pattern of other sizes are generated to cater to all shapes and sizes. Measurements will be marked "down" to generate the sizes "S" (small) and "XS" (extra small). Likewise, measurements will be marked "up" to create bigger sizes "L" and "XL" (large) and (extra-large) respectively. Accordingly, a measurement chart will be generated for the design houses review and confirmation.

A massive part of the pattern making process is carried out from the perspective of fabric consumption. From all the raw materials used in a garment, the yardages of fabrics utilized in a garment often contribute to a major cost of the garment. Therefore, a constant check on the fabric's consumption is essential. The art of the efficient pattern masters is to create patterns that are laid on the fabric is such a manner that maximizes the use of every inch of the fabric to minimize wastage. This process is called "lay-plan". They play with the length and sweep of the garments and try many different variations to use the least fabric. The width of the fabrics play an important role as the wider width accommodates more panels and reduces the multiple length required to make a complete garment.

The art of laying multiple size patterns on a fabric layer further allows the pattern masters to additionally reduce the fabric requirements. The fabric consumption has a direct impact as the pattern increases from

XXS (the smallest size) to XXL (the largest size). More centimeter square area is required to accommodate the incremental sizes. Considering the volume of size XXS which may have a consumption of 1.80 meters verses size XXL with a consumption going as high as 2.20 meters. It is common practice to average the fabric consumption by laying the biggest size along with the smallest size and accommodate the two sizes together on a fabric lay resulting in a consumption of 2 meters for each garment. Sometimes skillful and experienced pattern masters may further reduce the consumption by a few centimeters by adapting this method.

When the order quantity is high, every centimeter saved is a huge cost saving for the business. One centimeter saved per garment in an order quantity of ten thousand units is a hundred meters of fabric saved. You can do the math yourself to calculate the cost of a meter multiplying into meters saved. And imagine if the order consists of tens of thousands of units, the accumulated saving could be tenfold.

THE TEXTILE ENGINEERS AND COLOR CHEMISTS

While the patterns are getting ready, the sourcing team is busy gathering the materials and accessories to prepare the samples. At this stage the samples are normally made in substitute print and/ or color but in the right fabric quality, texture and weight to access the drape, flow, form, and silhouette of the garment.

As the samples are being generated, the sourcing team in parallel creates fabric quality samples, lab-dips for solid colors and strike-offs for prints.

The fabric quality samples are usually sent as a hanger from existing available yardages to confirm the fabric quality. Once the fabric quality samples are approved the manufacturer will place an order for the bulk fabric to one of its regular mills. Garment manufactures normally collaborate with a few mills, dyers and printing houses to build a long-term collaborative business relationship. This ensures their orders get priority and are completed on time since time is of the essence in the fast-moving fashion industry.

Since the color absorption, consistency and density is required to be evaluated, lab-dips are generated on strips in the accurate fabric quantity. Three to four options of lab-dips are prepared for each color to match with the target pantone color. The four cuttings will be variations of the target color with very slight differences. The lab-dips are generated in multiples for the purpose of evaluation and selection by the technologist. 2 x 2 inches of each option is attached onto a lab-dip submission sheet with all necessary details of the color mentioned on it.

There are several methods of fabric printing, however the most efficient and cost-effective method is screen print during the sampling stages. The print strike-offs take a long time to be created as it involves transferring the design onto a silk screen. This screen has micro pores in the areas where the color is pushed through with a squeezer to reach the surface of the fabric to form the print. Print strike-offs are usually submitted in an 8 x 8inch dimension on a print strike-off submission sheet but large format prints may need to be submitted on a bigger cutting which can display one design repeat.

THE FABRIC QUALITY EVALUATION

Before we dive into fabric evaluations, let me share the properties of the two primary textile types used in the industry, namely "Woven" and "Knitted" fabrics. Woven and knitted fabrics differ primarily in their construction and flexibility as explained below.

Woven Fabrics Construction Technique

Woven fabrics are made on a loom, where two sets of yarns (warp and weft) are interlaced perpendicularly. The warp yarns run lengthwise, while the weft yarns are threaded horizontally, creating a tight and stable fabric structure. While there are numerous weaving techniques to create intricate weave patterns, a few basic are listed below...

Plain Weave (e.g., cotton): Simple, durable, and widely used.

Twill Weave (e.g., denim): Diagonal texture, more durable with a high draping ability.

Satin Weave (e.g., satin): Smooth, glossy surface, often used in formal wear and bridal wear.

Woven fabrics have limited stretch, except on the bias (diagonal direction), giving them a firm feel that holds shape well. This makes them ideal for structured garments that need to keep their form, like tailored jackets, pants, and shirts.

Knitted Fabrics Construction Technique

Knitted fabrics are made by interlooping one or more yarns in a series of connected loops. This creates a stretchy, elastic fabric that can expand and contract. Knitting techniques are typically:

Weft Knitting (e.g., jersey): A single yarn forms rows of loops; common for soft, stretchable fabrics.

Warp Knitting (e.g., tricot): Multiple yarns form columns of loops, creating a more stable knit; used in active wear and lingerie.

Knits are naturally stretchy, comfortable, and conform to body movement, making them ideal for casual or fitted garments like t-shirts, leggings, and sportswear. They're softer and warmer compared to wovens, often used for clothing requiring flexibility and ease of movement.

Following are Key Differences in both fabric types

Stretch: Knitted fabrics offer natural elasticity, while woven fabrics are typically non-stretchy unless blended with elastane or cut on the bias.

Durability: Wovens tend to be more durable and abrasion-resistant, while knits provide comfort and adapt to the body shape.

Applications: Wovens suit structured, tailored apparel, while knits are favored for casual, form-fitting, or athletic clothing.

In summary, the main differences stem from construction, which affects the fabric's texture, durability, and suitability for various types of garments and the fabric evaluation process is carried out considering these properties.

THE EVALUATION PROCEDURE

In the garment business, fabric quality evaluation is a comprehensive procedure that includes visual inspections as well as technical tests to ensure materials fulfill design and performance standards. There are 4 crucial points to focus in evaluating a fabric quality submission:

The Fabric Quality: This includes assessing the overall durability, weave consistency, and finishing of the fabric. Look for defects like snags, color inconsistencies, or irregular textures that could affect the final garment's appearance and longevity. Quality checks help determine whether the fabric will withstand regular wear and care.

Color Matching: Color accuracy is crucial, especially when matching the fabric to other materials in a collection or against brand standards. Using a color card or swatch, compare the fabric under different lighting conditions to check for consistent hue, saturation, and vibrancy, ensuring it aligns with design specifications. Furthermore, the evaluation of a "lab-dip" (submissions of solid colors, or single colored fabrics) and "strike-off" (where colors are printed on part of the fabric or printed all over, usually covering the base fabric color) is explained below.

Fabric Weight Check: The weight of a fabric impacts the drape, structure, and suitability for certain garments. Measure the weight (grams per square meter or ounces per yard) to confirm it aligns with intended use—for instance, lightweight fabrics for summer wear or heavier materials for outerwear. This ensures the fabric will perform well in its intended garment.

Texture and Hand feel: Hand feel refers to the tactile quality of the fabric—how it feels to the touch. This can range from smooth and soft to rough or stiff, depending on the fabric's composition and finishing. Assessing hand feel helps determine whether the fabric will provide comfort, drape appropriately, and meet the intended sensory experience for the customer.

Evaluating each of these aspects carefully supports product consistency, quality control, and customer satisfaction in the final garment.

COLOR EVALUATION - LAB-DIP EVALUATION

The lab-dip evaluation procedure is a crucial step in the apparel industry's color approval process. It ensures that the fabric color matches the designer's desired shade and maintains color consistency across production batches. Here's a breakdown of the procedure:

i. Initial Submission: Fabric mills or dye houses create lab-dip samples by dyeing small fabric swatches to match the specified Pantone or color standard provided by the brand or designer.

ii. Submission and Evaluation: Lab-dips are submitted in several shades, known as "light, medium, and dark" versions, allowing options for selecting the closest match. These samples are evaluated under standard lighting conditions, often including daylight, fluorescent, and sometimes UV light, to simulate various real-life environments.

iii. Approval Process: The lab dips are inspected visually or with a spectrophotometer, which measures color accuracy by comparing the fabric color to the target color digitally. A small delta value indicates closer alignment, with lower values typically being acceptable.

iv. Feedback and Revisions: If lab-dips do not meet the standard, they are returned with specific feedback to the dye house for re-dyeing. This process may repeat until the lab-dip is approved.

v. Production Reference: Once approved, the lab-dip becomes the color standard for bulk production, ensuring all fabric produced aligns with the designer's vision.

Lab-dip evaluation is essential for achieving color consistency and quality, which are vital for brand integrity and customer satisfaction.

PRINTED FABRIC – STRIKE OFF EVALUATION

In addition to the standard lab-dip evaluation for color, evaluating printed fabric submissions involves two extra steps:

Print Scale Verification and Print Registration.

These checks ensure the quality, alignment, and aesthetic accuracy of the print design on the fabric. Here's an overview of each:

Print Scale

This step verifies that the size of the print matches the designer's intent and technical specifications. Any variation in the print scale can significantly impact the visual appeal and alignment of the print on the garment. Samples are measured to confirm that patterns (like florals, stripes, or graphics) appear proportionate and maintain consistency across the fabric.

Print Registration

Print registration assesses the alignment and positioning of each color layer within the print design. For multi-colored prints, each color is printed separately, making it essential to check that all layers align accurately without overlapping or leaving gaps. Poor registration can make the design look blurred or misaligned, which can affect the overall quality of the garment.

Both steps are crucial for maintaining the design integrity and visual appeal of printed fabrics in the final product.

THE SAMPLING CYCLE

The technological needs, complexity of the samples and the manufacturing facilities limitations determine the rounds of sample needed until satisfactory approval.

The "style and fit sample" also called a "first sample" is as the name suggests the very first sample of a constructed garment. This garment is required to be made in the accurate fabric quality, but could be in substitute color and print. The right quality of the fabric is needed to analyze the drape and fall of the fabric and its behavior in garment form. The garment is also required to be structured as defined in the technical brief. Measurement specification, pocket, collar, button placements must be accurate. The construction of seams when attaching together parts of the garment must be accurately followed as per guidelines to suit the fabric quality and to enhance the wearability and durability of the garment.

It is extremely important to use the right submission formats when submitting the items for evaluations. Each submission sheet is designed to fulfill the evaluation of a particular submission with its respective set of details and specifications. These details and specifications, no matter how minor, cannot be ignored. Overlooking these specifications may have severe consequences during the later stages of the product development process.

It is perfectly normal for the design house to ask for a revised sample which is termed as a "Second Fit Sample" in case on amendments or changes.

Every company may have a different set of forms to use. Some may merge a few forms together for speed and yet some may have an extensive cycle of submissions and approvals. Involving actual evaluators in the feedback process is essential for refining submission and evaluation formats. Their insights help ensure that critical details are covered, allowing for a more comprehensive and effective evaluation. Evaluators are in the best position to identify which aspects are crucial for assessing quality and which are not, making their input invaluable.

More importantly, this collaboration helps eliminate trivial points that unnecessarily extend evaluation time without adding value. By streamlining the process, evaluators can focus on what truly matters, leading to more accurate and efficient assessments. This not only enhances the quality of the evaluation but also saves time and resources, contributing to a more productive and focused evaluation process overall.

CHAPTER 4

EVERY PENNY COUNTS – SMART SOURCING

THE ART OF SOURCING

Every detail from the initial design stage to the finished product stage is significant. Therefore, sourcing excellent quality fabrics and materials is of paramount importance. The competitive edge for any fast fashion retailer is to capitalize on speed and cost making their merchandise easily available to the masses. These brands liaise with their manufacturers to quickly produce the required quantities of renegotiated cost-effective materials and production procedures enabling them to retail fashionable clothing at competitive prices. The fast fashion stores are the go-to places for customers looking for current trends at affordable prices.

Fast fashion stores operate on a tight timescale to remain competitive and maximize current trends. Their product development cycle is designed to build efficiency and speed allowing them to swiftly offer new styles to the customers. Fast fashion adapts to a competitive pricing strategy to make fashion more affordable to budget-conscious consumers looking for value fashion and variety. Their marketing and promotional activities highlight affordability, diversity, and variety attracting all classes of customers.

Maintaining the appropriate balance between customer satisfaction, timelines, and budgets, the sourcing team embarks on a quest to get the right product from the right supplier. The buyers dive into the pool of loyal suppliers and sometimes find new suppliers to indulge in negotiations on costs and timelines. The buyers are the administrators who lead the conversations and are the point of contact with the manufacturers ensuring momentum and speed as per established dates and milestones on the critical path.

It is a key performance indicator for a buyer to collaborate and liaise with the extended teams and departments internally and externally. They are responsible for ensuring the goods arrive in the warehouses for allocation to stores in time for the seasonal launch. They need to work with the specialized teams for expert opinions ensuring submissions and approvals are received, issued, and released within the agreed duration.

We will discuss more on the critical path, key performance indicators, standard operating procedures, and communication in the upcoming chapters.

COSTING STRATEGY

The art of negotiation is the core skill of a buyer. Fashion buyers use multiple complex approaches to lower costs without impacting product quality. Cost efficiency is a continuous effort critical to a business's long-term profitability and growth in the constantly evolving fashion environment. Buyers efficiently negotiate discounts based on volumes, winning advantageous conditions using their purchasing power. Mutually beneficial relationships cultivated by the buyers aid in building beneficial partnerships while reducing costs and improving efficiency leading to shared success.

Cleaver sourcing practices encourage buyers to research and compare rates from multiple suppliers while watching out for currency conversion rate swings. This practice allowed buyers to make calculated and informed decisions to get the best deals, reduce currency risks, and increase purchasing power. Ensuring the internal process efficiency and minimizing overheads substantially helps in controlling costs demonstrating excellent economic discipline without compromising quality.

From material optimization to upgrading manufacturing practices, every stage of the value chain is analyzed for continuous improvement to achieve long-term savings. Fashion buyers therefore perform frequent cost audits comparing season on season and year on year to identify alternate sourcing strategies or consolidate orders to lower costs and increase supply chain efficiency.

The accuracy of stock allocations in the right quantities to the right locations is vital in the success of achieving sales targets. Continuous monitoring for stock levels and consolidating stocks in high-selling stores ensures a healthy sales curve. Additionally, strong forecasting strategies and striking the right balance of supply to demand minimizes the risk of excess purchases leading to overstock of inventory or less than required purchases resulting in zero stocks.

TIME IS OF THE ESSENCE

Accurate planning and proactive management are skills required to organize effective and smooth product delivery in the fast-paced world of a fashion retail business. Several strategic steps are implemented to ensure timely product availability. Setting crystal clear expectations in terms of time frame and milestones is crucial in maintaining the pace of activities from initiation to completion of projects.

Critical Path Analysis (CPA) is an essential tool for any business with specific milestone deadlines. It is particularly useful when these milestones consist of multiple sub-activities that must be completed to achieve the overall goal. Continuous monitoring of production progress is critical to this endeavor, allowing purchasers to identify possible bottlenecks and address them ahead of time. Buyers use excellent communication channels to achieve deadline alignment with suppliers, promoting a shared commitment to reaching delivery targets. Recognizing the inherent dangers of supply chain dependency, buyers welcome diversification, purchasing from several regions to reduce the impact of interruptions.

Using technology, fashion buyers adopt supply chain visibility technologies for real-time tracking, increasing transparency and agility throughout the value chain. Furthermore, the formulation of contingency plans is a cornerstone of risk mitigation, allowing purchasers to traverse unexpected problems with resilience. Building strong relationships with logistics partners strengthens the delivery ecosystem by enabling efficient transportation and reducing transit times.

Strategic inventory management emerges as a critical component in delivery optimization efforts, as buyers attempt to reduce lead times while maintaining product availability. Buyers may uncover efficiencies by leveraging technology for supply chain automation and optimization, which reduces costs and increases responsiveness. Regular performance assessments with suppliers create an opportunity for productive communication, allowing buyers to address delivery concerns quickly and effectively. Fashion firms use this multidimensional strategy to orchestrate a symphony of efficiency and dependability, ensuring that products arrive at the intended destinations on time.

SUPPLIER RELIABILITY

In the complex web of fashion supply chains, the basis of success is the careful selection and maintenance of supplier relationships. Before entering into commercial agreements, fashion buyers perform extensive due diligence. This comprehensive vetting procedure includes reviewing supplier references and completing background checks to ensure compatibility with the brand's vision and values. Buyers build the framework for mutually successful, transparent, and accountable collaborations by establishing explicit expectations and commitments in supplier contracts.

Once contracts have been created, the journey continues with close monitoring of supplier performance via key performance indicators (KPIs). These indicators act as compass points, leading customers and suppliers toward common goals. Beyond numbers, however, lies the heart of partnership-building, which is founded on trust and open communication. Buyers establish relationships that go beyond transactional exchanges by cultivating an environment of collaboration and mutual respect, resulting in a culture of shared success.

However, given the dynamic landscape of supply chain management, readiness is critical. Fashion buyers build contingency plans to limit the impact of supplier failures or disruptions, to protect against unexpected obstacles. Buyers often maintain a "Supplier Management & Evaluation Program" to monitor supplier performance over time. Suppliers are graded according to their performance and ranked based on their comprehensive services against set criteria. Furthermore, buyers recognize the importance of consistent performance and promote excellence with long-term contracts or performance bonuses. However, the goal of dependability goes beyond incentives; buyers invest in supplier development programs, which promote ongoing improvement and resilience throughout the supply chain.

Furthermore, the commitment to quality includes frequent audits of supplier facilities and processes to ensure adherence to standards and regulations. Buyers embrace variety by implementing supplier diversification initiatives, which reduce the risks associated with reliance on a single supplier. Buyers strengthen their supply chains by building a wide network of suppliers, allowing them to navigate uncertainty with agility and adaptability. Through these comprehensive efforts, fashion brands form ties that go beyond transactions, expressing a shared dedication to excellence and innovation.

QUALITY

In the dynamic and rapidly changing world of fashion, keeping flawless product quality is critical to brand reputation and customer pleasure. To do this, fashion houses have regular quality checks performed at supplier facilities, ensuring that every step of the manufacturing process meets strict criteria. Implementing quality control measures is a commitment to excellence that begins with the sourcing of raw materials and ends with the final packaging.

The creation of precise quality standards and specifications for each product is critical to this effort. These rules serve as the foundation of quality assurance activities, providing buyers and suppliers with a road map for maintaining the brand's integrity. Furthermore, buyers understand the value of continual feedback loops, which provide constructive insights to suppliers for continued improvement. This collaborative approach promotes a culture of quality and creativity, propelling product progress toward perfection.

In concert with these efforts, stringent product testing processes are implemented to assess durability, performance, and safety. Each stitch, seam, and fabric choice is meticulously scrutinized, guaranteeing that only the best products reach the discerning buyer. Compliance with industry quality certifications reinforces the commitment to excellence, instilling confidence in consumers and stakeholders. Further emphasis on quality is discussed in detail in the later chapters on quality management.

The customer's voice continues to be a guiding beacon on this journey to quality excellence. Fashion houses stay on top of changing preferences and expectations by closely monitoring client feedback and responding to any quality issues as soon as possible. However, the pursuit of quality goes beyond just observation; it requires direct engagement and empowerment. Thus, suppliers receive comprehensive training on quality management best practices, promoting a shared commitment to great craftsmanship.

Crucially, developing long-term partnerships with reputable suppliers known for their commitment to quality is essential. These collaborations go beyond economic transactions, demonstrating a mutual commitment to raising standards. Furthermore, fashion brands recognize the critical role of technology and invest in cutting-edge solutions to improve quality control and monitoring. Fashion brands continue to set the standard for quality in an ever-changing market by bringing together knowledge, innovation, and steadfast dedication.

SUSTAINABILITY

In the dynamic ecosystem of fashion supply chains, sustainability has developed as a guiding principle, influencing procurement strategies. Corporates understand the critical role that suppliers play in achieving long-term change and actively seek connections with organizations that share their values. By prioritizing engagement with suppliers who have established sustainability efforts, buyers build the framework for a shared path toward environmental stewardship and social responsibility.

The strict implementation of environmental regulations, aided by regular audits to ensure vendors adhere to sustainable practices, is central to this effort. These audits serve as a litmus test, confirming suppliers' commitment to decreasing their environmental impact and adopting eco-friendly practices. Buyers actively urge suppliers to reduce waste and implement creative solutions that enhance resource efficiency and conservation.

Furthermore, the desire for sustainability pervades the fundamental fabric of sourcing decisions, with purchasers prioritizing materials derived from renewable or recycled sources. Buyers who adhere to circular economy principles not only reduce their environmental effect, but also help to preserve precious resources. Buyers also promote fair trade and ethical labor policies, ensuring that the human dimension of sustainability is kept throughout the supply chain.

Buyers, in parallel with sourcing methods, lead activities to redesign packaging solutions, advocating for the adoption of sustainable alternatives that reduce environmental harm. Buyers actively participate in educational activities, providing suppliers with the knowledge and resources they need to get started on their sustainability path. By measuring and reporting on sustainability measures, buyers promote accountability and transparency, establishing a culture of continuous improvement and shared responsibility.

Furthermore, brands actively participate in industry-wide programs that promote sustainability and use collective action to achieve systemic change. Buyers reward and prioritize sustainable practices by including sustainability targets in supplier contracts and assessments, so embedding sustainability into the very fabric of procurement processes. Fashion buyers use their collective influence to guide the industry toward a more sustainable and fair future.

INNOVATIVE TENDENCY

In the ever-changing fashion scene, innovation reigns supreme, driving the pulse of creativity and dictating the trajectory of trends. Fashion buyers are at the forefront of this innovation, orchestrating a symphony of collaboration, discovery, and experimentation that propels the industry forward. At the center of this effort is a mutually beneficial cooperation between buyers and suppliers, in which collaboration on product development and design serves as the foundation for innovation. Buyers leverage suppliers' collaborative creativity by encouraging open avenues of communication and idea exchange, pouring new perspectives into every stitch and silhouette.

Furthermore, buyers actively connect with the fashion industry's broader ecosystem, attending trade exhibitions and networking events to learn about new suppliers and developing trends. These forums act as crucibles of inspiration, allowing buyers to gain insights and make connections that spark innovation and strategic partnerships. However, the desire for innovation goes beyond simply observation; brands invest in sophisticated R&D activities to uncover emerging trends and anticipate altering consumer preferences. By staying ahead of the curve, buyers establish themselves as tastemakers, expertly navigating the ever-changing currents of fashion.

Consumer-centricity is crucial to innovation, as buyers perform extensive research to understand their target audience's varied tastes and wants. With these insights, buyers can cultivate creativity and encourage calculated risk-taking in product design and development, empowering teams to challenge traditions and redefine the status quo. Furthermore, purchasers capitalize on the attraction of exclusivity by delivering limited-edition products that create a sense of urgency and desire among customers. This strategic route not only cultivates brand loyalty but also develops a culture of anticipation and excitement in the marketplace.

Buyers keep a close eye on rival activity and industry trends, getting inspiration from the zeitgeist while navigating their own distinctive path of innovation. In a congested marketplace, buyers assure relevance and resonance by soliciting customer feedback and applying it into product creation. Buyers also encourage experimentation, investigating new materials, technologies, and manufacturing processes to push the limits of potential. By relentlessly pursuing innovation, buyers foster a culture of creativity and ingenuity within their businesses and among their suppliers, establishing the framework for a future distinguished by bold ideas and breakthroughs.

FLEXIBILITY

Fashion brands quest to cater to the ever-changing consumer needs, agility reigns supreme as buyers negotiate a terrain fraught with change and unpredictability. The preservation of open lines of communication with suppliers is critical to this endeavor, as is the promotion of a collaborative and responsive culture. By keeping communication channels open, buyers promote speedy decision-making, allowing both sides to adjust quickly to changing conditions and exploit opportunities as they emerge.

Furthermore, buyers understand the importance of having agile supply chain procedures that can navigate the market's ebbs and flows. This requires developing partnerships with numerous suppliers, diversifying sourcing choices to reduce risk, and strengthening the supply chain's resilience to interruptions. By embracing flexibility as a cornerstone of supply chain management, buyers create a dynamic ecosystem capable of weathering the storm of uncertainty.

Crucially, technology promotes agility by providing purchasers with real-time data analysis and forecasting capabilities. Investing in cutting-edge technologies, such as smart inventory management systems, gives buyers the flexibility to make educated decisions and pivot rapidly in reaction to market changes.

Furthermore, implementing contingency measures, such as alternative sourcing choices and safety stock, strengthens the supply chain and ensures continuity in the face of adversity.

Recognizing that agility is as much about people as it is about processes, brands invest in employee training to provide teams with problem-solving capabilities and decision-making abilities in dynamic circumstances. Brands also promote collaboration and creativity by forming cross-functional teams and departments, leveraging the pooled expertise of multiple viewpoints to face unforeseen difficulties head-on.

Furthermore, brands perform frequent inspections of supply chain procedures to find areas for development and process efficiency. This dedication to continual improvement demonstrates a willingness to change, as brands continue to look for ways to improve the supply chain's efficiency and effectiveness. This iterative strategy helps buyers not only negotiate the complexity of the fashion world, but also construct a route to long-term success in an ever-changing sector.

TRANSPARENCY

Fashion buyers understand the critical relevance of delivering clear and accurate information to suppliers about their expectations and requirements. Buyers establish the groundwork for successful collaborations with the supply base grounded on mutual understanding and alignment by outlining their demands and standards from the start.

Furthermore, buyers value open communication with stakeholders, exchanging insights and decisions about sourcing procedures. By promoting transparency in decision-making processes, both parties build a culture of trust and collaboration, allowing stakeholders to make significant contributions to strategic projects.

Crucially, buyers take a collaborative approach with suppliers, exchanging pertinent data and insights to promote innovation and efficiency. Buyers empower suppliers by creating avenues for feedback and communication, allowing them to express their problems, make suggestions, and actively participate in problem resolution initiatives.

Transparency extends beyond internal operations; buyers are dedicated to being open about their sourcing procedures with customers and the public. Buyers that provide transparency into the origins and processes of their products not only increase brand reputation, but also empower consumers to make informed decisions that align with their values.

In the spirit of openness, buyers hold regular supplier meetings and updates, promoting an open communication and accountability culture. Furthermore, buyers supply vendors with knowledge and tools to help them enhance their performance, building a mutually beneficial relationship based on success.

Maintaining trust and credibility requires open and honest communication with stakeholders about their issues or inquiries. Buyers demonstrate their commitment to responsible practices by establishing publicly published codes of conduct or ethical sourcing policies.

Furthermore, purchasers frequently participate in industry-wide transparency programs or certifications, demonstrating a commitment to sustaining the highest levels of integrity and accountability. Through these collaborative efforts, fashion buyers not only negotiate the complexity of the supply chain, but also pave the way for a more transparent and sustainable future for the entire industry.

COMPLIANCE & RISK MANAGEMENT

Compliance with regulations and standards is critical in the complex functions of fashion supply chains to maintain integrity and reduce risks. Fashion buyers stay up to date on industry norms and standards, realizing that legal requirements change all the time in the geographical regions of their commercial activities. This proactive approach is supplemented by regular audits to ensure suppliers meet these legal responsibilities. Buyers that perform thorough inspections demonstrate their commitment to ethical sourcing procedures and protect themselves from potential risks.

Furthermore, buyers play a critical role in providing suppliers with the knowledge and tools they need to navigate compliance concerns efficiently. Providing compliance training and tools not only promotes a responsible culture, but it also enhances the supply chain's resistance to regulatory issues. Furthermore, buyers provide explicit standards and expectations in supplier contracts, creating the framework for open and accountable collaborations.

Collaboration with legal and regulatory specialists is critical for maintaining compliance across the supply chain. Buyers receive insights into developing regulatory landscapes and can solve compliance gaps more proactively by leveraging specialized expertise. Buyers also put in place internal controls and monitoring processes to ensure standards are met and deviations are detected early on.

Compliance requires rigorous record-keeping for traceability and accountability. Buyers keep extensive records of sourcing operations, which improves transparency and auditability. Furthermore, buyers respond quickly to any compliance violations or difficulties, taking immediate corrective action to reduce risks and maintain ethical standards.

Buyers perform detailed risk assessments to identify potential hazards because they understand how linked issues are inside the supply chain. Buyers develop risk mitigation strategies and contingency plans to offset the negative effects of supplier failures and geopolitical instability. Diversifying sourcing regions and building relationships with alternative suppliers serve as buffers against concentration risk, ensuring continuity in the face of potential disruptions.

Furthermore, buyers use digital solutions to improve supply chain visibility and risk management. Buyers who invest in advanced tools obtain insights into potential vulnerabilities and may manage risks more proactively. Furthermore, buyers work with partners along the supply chain to handle shared risks jointly, encouraging resilience and adaptation in a constantly changing environment. Fashion buyers work together to tackle the complexity of compliance and risk management, ensuring the supply chain's integrity and sustainability.

CHAPTER 5

THREADS OF THE WORLD – MANUFACTURING INSIGHTS

GEOGRAPHICAL POSITIONING

The geographical distribution of fashion manufacturing hubs is influenced by several factors, including labor costs, infrastructure, trade policies, and market demand. Historically, countries such as China, Bangladesh, Vietnam, and India have been key manufacturing hubs due to their large labor force and low salaries. These countries have created textile and apparel industries that are supported by large supply chains, giving them a competitive advantage in mass production.

China, in particular, has been a dominant force in global fashion industry, being the world's largest supplier of textiles and garments. Its size, efficiency, and manufacturing capabilities have made it a top choice for many firms looking for cost-effective production. However, rising labor prices, currency volatility, and trade disputes have pushed some corporations to shift their manufacturing base to other Southeast Asian nations, such as Vietnam and Bangladesh, which provide comparable benefits at lower rates.

In recent years, there has also been a shift toward reshoring or nearshoring manufacturing closer to consumer markets. This movement tries to reduce the lead time, shipping expenses, and supply chain hazards associated with offshore manufacturing. Countries in Eastern Europe, such as Turkey, Romania, and Poland, have emerged as desirable places for fashion manufacture due to their talented workforce, closeness to major European markets, and favorable trade agreements.

Furthermore, Africa and Latin America are emerging as attractive fashion production destinations, thanks to factors such as advantageous trade agreements, government incentives, and a rising pool of young, trainable labor. Countries such as Ethiopia, Kenya, and Morocco in Africa, as well as Mexico, Peru, and Colombia in Latin America, are drawing investment from worldwide brands and retailers seeking to diversify their sourcing strategies and enter new consumer markets.

Overall, the geographical distribution of production hubs in the fashion industry is fluid and changing, influenced by a variety of economic, social, and geopolitical factors. While traditional Asian manufacturing locations remain vital, there is a growing tendency toward diversification and regionalization to manage risks and capitalize on emerging opportunities in various regions of the globe.

OUTSOURCING & GLOBAL SUPPLY CHAINS

Outsourcing and global supply chains are critical to the fashion industry's operations, allowing brands and retailers to access a wide selection of suppliers, resources, and production capacity throughout the world. This decentralized production model has various advantages, including lower costs, greater flexibility, and access to specialist skills and technologies.

However, managing global supply chains presents major hurdles, notably in terms of supply chain visibility, openness, and adherence to labor and environmental standards. The intricate network of suppliers and subcontractors engaged in garment manufacturing can make it challenging for businesses to monitor and maintain ethical and sustainable standards throughout the supply chain.

Efforts to increase transparency and sustainability in the fashion supply chain have resulted in the creation of a number of programs and standards. These projects seek to encourage responsible sourcing, labor rights, and environmental stewardship by providing tools, guidelines, and certification schemes for brands and manufacturers to evaluate and improve their supply chain operations.

Furthermore, technological innovations like blockchain, RFID tagging, and digital traceability platforms allow for better transparency and traceability in fashion supply chains. These technologies enable firms to follow the course of items from raw materials to finished goods, informing customers about the origins, manufacturing methods, and environmental impact of their purchases.

Despite these efforts, there are still hurdles to guaranteeing ethical and ecological standards throughout the fashion supply chain. Worker exploitation, environmental degradation, and waste are all ongoing issues, underscoring the need for increased collaboration and accountability among industry players to address these systemic concerns.

The fashion industry relies significantly on outsourcing and global supply networks to sustain its operations, as these enable international trade, foster innovation, and enhance market access. To tackle complex challenges and drive meaningful change, ethical and sustainable supply chain practices must be upheld through ongoing commitment and collaboration across the sector.

TECHNOLOGY AND AUTOMATION

One of the most important trends in fashion manufacturing is the use of automation and robotics to expedite production processes and save labor expenses.

Automation technology, such as computerized cutting machines, robotic sewing systems, and automated warehouse systems, allow for faster production, higher precision, and more consistent product quality. These technologies also help to reduce dependency on human labor, especially for repetitive, labor-intensive complicated steps, or hazardous jobs, resulting in better working conditions and more productivity.

Another source of innovation in fashion production is the use of digital tools and technologies for design and prototyping. Computer-aided design (CAD) software, 3D modeling applications, and virtual prototype platforms enable designers to develop and view garments in a digital environment, accelerating design iteration and minimizing the need for real samples in some cases. This not only saves time and costs, but also allows for more creativity and experimentation in design.

Furthermore, technologies such as 3D prints and additive manufacturing are transforming the way fashion products are manufactured, enabling on-demand production, customization, and waste reduction. 3D printing allows for the development of complicated geometries and elaborate designs that would be difficult or impossible to produce using standard manufacturing processes. This adaptability and diversity create new opportunities for product invention and personalization, according to individual tastes and preferences.

Aside from automation and digitization, advances in materials science and sustainable technologies are driving innovation in garment manufacturing. Sustainable materials, including recycled fibers, bio-based textiles, and alternative leather replacements, are gaining popularity as manufacturers strive to lessen their environmental impact while meeting consumer demand for eco-friendly products. Similarly, technologies such as waterless dyeing, zero-waste pattern cutting, and closed-loop recycling enable more environmentally friendly and resource-efficient manufacturing methods.

Overall, technology and automation are transforming the fashion business, providing the potential to improve efficiency, quality, and sustainability across the entire manufacturing process. However, widespread adoption of these technologies necessitates investment, infrastructure, and workforce upskilling to reach their full potential and address the issues of the modern fashion business.

SUSTAINABILITY AND ETHICAL PRACTICES

Sustainability and ethical standards have grown in importance in the fashion business as consumers become more conscious of environmental and social issues. The old linear model of fashion production, which involves the rapid consumption and disposal of garments, has resulted in severe environmental deterioration, such as resource depletion, pollution, and waste. In response, there is a rising push for more sustainable and responsible methods throughout the fashion value chain.

One significant area of concentration is materials innovation, with brands and manufacturers looking into alternative fibers, recycled materials, and organic fabrics to lessen the environmental effect of garment production. Recycled polyester, for example, is made from post-consumer plastic bottles, whereas organic cotton is farmed without synthetic pesticides or fertilizers, which reduces water use and chemical pollution. Similarly, advances in biodegradable and bio-based materials present interesting alternatives to typical petroleum-based synthetics, with materials such as mushroom leather, cactus leather, and pineapple fiber earning attention for their environmental credentials.

Furthermore, fashion firms and suppliers are increasingly concerned with sustainable manufacturing techniques such as water and energy saving, waste minimization, and pollution prevention. Technologies such as waterless dyeing, which reduces the need for vast amounts of water in the dyeing process, and closed-loop recycling, which recycles post-consumer textiles into new fabrics, are helping to reduce the environmental effect of textile manufacturing.

In addition to environmental concerns, the fashion industry is constantly investigated for labor working conditions in factories and garment supply networks. Child labor, forced labor, and unsafe working conditions are still prevalent in many manufacturing hubs, particularly in developing nations with lax labor standards and inadequate enforcement systems. Many brands globally adapt ethical sourcing initiatives, such as fair-trade certification, social compliance audits, and worker empowerment programs, to raise labor standards and assure fair salaries, safe working conditions, and worker rights across the supply chain.

Furthermore, transparency and traceability are critical components of sustainability and ethical fashion, allowing customers to make educated decisions about the items they purchase and the businesses they support. Many businesses are promoting supply chain openness by exposing supplier lists, publishing factory audit reports, and including information about their environmental and social effect on product labels and websites. This transparency fosters confidence and accountability among consumers and stakeholders, increasing demand for ethically made and transparently sourced fashion products.

Sustainability and ethical practices are critical to the future of the fashion industry, as businesses acknowledge the importance of balancing economic growth with environmental care and social responsibility. Fashion firms can reduce their environmental impact, increase worker wellbeing, and create a more resilient and responsible sector for the future by implementing sustainable materials, production techniques, and supply chain policies.

DIGITAL TRANSFORMATION

The fashion industry's digital transformation has intensified in recent years, transforming how companies design, manufacture, market, and sell garments and accessories. From virtual fashion shows to AI-powered recommendation engines, digital technologies are propelling innovation and disruption throughout the fashion value chain.

One of the most significant effects of digital transformation is in the field of electronic commerce. The rise of Internet shopping platforms has transformed the way consumers discover and buy fashion products, enabling increased convenience, choice, and accessibility. With the spread of smartphones and internet access, consumers can shop whenever, wherever, and from a diverse selection of brands and merchants, removing conventional entry barriers and boosting fashion firms' exposure to worldwide markets.

Furthermore, digital technologies are influencing how fashion products are planned and developed. Computer-aided design (CAD) software and 3D modeling technologies enable designers to construct virtual prototypes and mimic garments in a digital environment, minimizing the need for actual samples and expediting the design iteration process. This not only saves time and costs, but also allows for greater creativity and experimentation in design, resulting in more inventive and sustainable products.

Furthermore, digital technologies are transforming how fashion products are advertised and promoted to consumers. Social media sites such as Instagram, TikTok, and Pinterest have become critical outlets for fashion firms to communicate with their customers, display new collections, and increase engagement and sales. Influencer marketing, in which social media influencers and content creators recommend things to their followers, has evolved as a significant strategy for brand promotion and customer acquisition, taking use of influencers' trust and authenticity to efficiently reach target audiences.

Furthermore, advances in augmented reality (AR) and virtual reality (VR) are providing immersive and interactive shopping experiences, allowing customers to see and try on clothing virtually before making a purchase. Virtual fitting rooms, augmented reality try-on apps, and digital styling services offer individualized advice and improve the online shopping experience, lowering returns and increasing consumer happiness.

Furthermore, data analytics and artificial intelligence (AI) are helping fashion firms acquire insights into consumer preferences, behaviors, and trends, allowing them to make data-driven decisions and optimize their marketing and merchandising strategies. AI-powered recommendation engines, predictive analytics, and tailored marketing campaigns enable brands to provide relevant and personalized shopping experiences to individual customers, hence increasing engagement, loyalty, and revenue.

Finally, digital transformation is changing the fashion sector by challenging established business models and transforming how items are conceived, manufactured, marketed, and sold. By embracing digital technologies and innovation, fashion brands and retailers can stay ahead of the curve, satisfy consumers' changing wants and expectations, and establish more resilient and sustainable businesses in an increasingly digital environment.

CHAPTER 6

INSIGHTFUL OBSERVATIONS – SAMPLE ASSESSMENT

EVALUATION SIGNIFICANCE

Evaluations in the sample process are essential to bridge the gap between initial design concepts and final production-ready garments. By meticulously assessing each sample, teams can identify and address any discrepancies in fabric quality, fit, and construction, ensuring that the product meets the desired standards before mass production. This thorough examination reduces the risk of costly errors, maintains brand quality, and builds confidence that the final product will meet customer expectations and industry standards. In short, evaluations are the key to refining ideas into market-ready designs with precision and purpose.

INITIAL VISUAL REVIEW OF DESIGN ASSESSMENT

Performing a visual check on a submitted sample for design verification is a crucial step in ensuring that the final product aligns with the original design specifications and meets quality standards. The first aspect to verify is the color match. Ensuring the sample's color corresponds accurately to the Pantone color reference used during the design phase is essential. This involves examining the sample under different lighting conditions to confirm consistency and precision in color reproduction, as any deviation can significantly impact the product's aesthetic and marketability.

The alignment of patterns, especially for prints or stripes, should be meticulously examined. Pattern alignment is vital for maintaining visual coherence and overall appeal. Misaligned patterns can make a product look unprofessional and diminish its perceived quality. This means checking seams, hems, and other junctions to ensure that patterns flow seamlessly across different parts of the garment. A well-aligned pattern not only enhances the visual appeal but also reflects the brand's commitment to quality and attention to detail.

It is crucial to confirm that all design elements such as embroidery, embellishments, or appliqués are correctly placed and executed. This step involves scrutinizing the sample for the accuracy and quality of these elements. Each piece of embroidery or embellishment should be securely attached, correctly positioned, and crafted to meet the design specifications. Inaccurate placement or poor execution can detract from the overall design, potentially harming the product's reception in the market.

Comparing the physical sample to the digital design files or sketches is essential for identifying any discrepancies. This comparison ensures that the sample faithfully represents the intended design, allowing for the detection and correction of any deviations early in the production process. Moreover, the overall aesthetic appeal should be reviewed, considering the brand's identity and current market trends. This holistic review ensures the product not only meets technical specifications but also resonates with the target audience, aligning with both brand values and consumer expectations. By performing a thorough visual check, the product team can ensure that the final product is both high-quality and visually appealing, enhancing its success in the marketplace.

INITIAL VISUAL REVIEW CONSTRUCTION CHECK

Performing a visual check on a submitted sample for construction quality is essential to ensure that the garment meets durability standards and provides a seamless finish. The first critical aspect to inspect is the consistency and neatness of stitching throughout the garment. Each seam should exhibit uniformity in stitching in the required stitches per inch (SPI), with straight lines and no loose threads, indicating skilled craftsmanship and attention to detail. Inconsistencies in stitching can compromise the garment's structural integrity and overall aesthetic.

Equally important is ensuring that seams are securely finished to prevent fraying or unraveling over time. A thorough examination of seam allowances and edges should confirm that they are adequately stitched and possibly reinforced where necessary. This step not only enhances the garment's longevity but also reflects quality manufacturing standards.

Checking for uniformity in stitch length and tension is another vital component of the construction check. Proper stitch length and tension contribute to the garment's strength and comfort. Irregularities in stitch length or tension can create puckering and weak spots that may compromise the garment's durability and comfort during wear. Therefore, a consistent and well-maintained stitching pattern is crucial for ensuring overall quality.

Assessing the placement and reinforcement of stress points such as buttonholes and pockets is also crucial. These areas undergo significant strain during use and must be reinforced accordingly to prevent tearing or damage. Buttonholes should be cleanly cut and sewn with sturdy stitching, while pockets should be securely attached and reinforced at the edges to withstand daily wear and tear.

Verifying that hems, cuffs, and other edges are cleanly finished and correctly measured completes the construction check. Neatly finished edges not only enhance the garment's appearance but also indicate precision in manufacturing. Properly measured hems and cuffs ensure uniformity in fit and length, contributing to the overall comfort and aesthetic appeal of the garment.

Conducting a visual check based on these construction criteria ensures that the submitted sample meets high-quality standards in both craftsmanship and durability. By focusing on stitching consistency, seam finishing, stitch quality, stress point reinforcement, and edge finishing, manufacturers can deliver garments that not only look impeccable but also stand the test of time, satisfying customer expectations for quality and longevity.

MEASUREMENT VERIFICATION FOR SIZE AND FIT

Performing measurement verification on a submitted garment sample is a critical step in ensuring quality and adherence to specifications before freezing base size patterns and generating lower and upper size grading. This process involves meticulous attention to detail to confirm that the garment's size and fit meet the required standards.

Upon receiving the garment sample, the product team in charge of sample evaluation initiates the verification process by carefully comparing the measurements provided in the specifications with those of the actual sample. Each measurement point—

from chest and waist circumference to sleeve length and inseam—is scrutinized to verify accuracy. This step is crucial as even minor deviations can impact the garment's fit, overall quality and impacts the garment fabric consumption. By meticulously measuring multiple points on the garment, we ensure that the size and fit align precisely with the intended design and customer expectations.

Any discrepancies identified during the measurement verification are carefully documented and communicated to the production teams. This feedback loop is essential for addressing potential issues early in the process, thereby minimizing the risk of producing garments that do not meet size and fit standards. Whether the differences are due to human errors in measurement or variations in manufacturing, our goal is to rectify these issues promptly to maintain consistency and quality across all garment samples.

Beyond numerical measurements, our verification process includes a physical evaluation of the garment's fit on a standardized dress form or live model where applicable. This step provides additional insights into how the garment drapes and conforms to body proportions. It allows us to assess not only the numerical measurements but also the practical aspects of comfort, movement, and overall aesthetic appeal. The ease of putting on and taking off the garment is also considered and monitored. This aspect not only relates to practical usability but also influences the overall comfort and user experience. Assessing how smoothly the garment can be worn and removed helps to gauge its functionality and suitability for everyday use. This holistic approach ensures that the garment not only fits according to size specifications but also meets subjective criteria related to comfort and style.

Lastly, upon successful completion of the measurement verification and fit assessment, detailed reports are provided to the manufacturers outlining the findings and any adjustments made. This transparency and documentation are crucial for maintaining clear communication throughout the production process and ensuring that all parties involved are aligned on the final specifications before full-scale production begins.

In conclusion, performing a measurement verification on a submitted garment sample is a meticulous process that combines precision measurement techniques with practical fit assessments. By adhering to strict standards and thorough documentation, we ensure that each garment meets the desired size and fit requirements, thereby upholding quality and customer satisfaction in every production cycle.

WEAR TRIAL FOR FUNCTIONAL COMFORT ASSESSMENT

Performing a fitting test evaluation focused on comfort assessment is essential to ensure that a garment not only fits well but also feels comfortable for prolonged wear in various conditions. This evaluation process integrates several critical components to comprehensively assess the comfort level of the garment.

Individuals are required to wear the garment for extended periods during the evaluation process. This step allows the evaluator to observe how the garment performs over time and assess its comfort during prolonged wear. By wearing the garment in real-world conditions, we can identify any discomfort or issues that may arise after extended use, ensuring that the garment remains comfortable throughout its intended lifespan.

Testing the garment in various dynamic conditions provides valuable insights into its material performance, particularly in terms of breathability and moisture management. Evaluating how well the fabric regulates temperature and moisture absorption helps determine its suitability for different climates and activities, enhancing overall comfort.

Evaluating the feel of the fabric against the skin is crucial to identifying any potential irritation or discomfort. We pay close attention to how the fabric texture and seams interact with the skin, ensuring that the garment's construction minimizes friction and enhances comfort, particularly in sensitive areas.

Assessing the garment's ability to maintain its shape and appearance after wear is another key aspect of comfort evaluation. We examine whether the garment stretches out of shape, wrinkles excessively, or retains its original appearance and structure. Maintaining the garment's integrity contributes to both comfort and aesthetic appeal over time.

Gathering subjective feedback from individuals wearing the garment is integral to the evaluation process. We seek their opinions on overall comfort and fit during various activities, such as walking, sitting, and exercising. This feedback provides qualitative insights into comfort levels that complement quantitative measurements, ensuring a well-rounded assessment.

In conclusion, conducting a user comfort assessment involves a comprehensive approach that considers prolonged wear, material performance in different climates, skin sensitivity, garment durability, and user feedback. By integrating these components, we ensure that each garment not only fits well but also meets high standards of comfort, enhancing the wearer's experience. This commitment to comfort assessment underscores our dedication to delivering garments that prioritize both functionality and user satisfaction across diverse environments and activities.

WEAR TRIAL FOR FUNCTIONAL PERFORMANCE ASSESSMENT

A performance assessment ensures that a garment not only fits well but also meets practical requirements for durability, functionality, and ease of maintenance. This evaluation process involves rigorous testing across various parameters to gauge the garment's performance during daily use.

Firstly, conducting stretch tests on fabrics such as knits is crucial to assess their elasticity and recovery. By subjecting the garment to controlled stretching, we evaluate how well the fabric maintains its shape and elasticity over repeated use. This test is essential for ensuring that the garment retains its fit and comfort, particularly in garments designed for active wear or everyday use.

Secondly, simulating everyday movements like bending and reaching helps us evaluate the garment's ease of motion. This dynamic assessment ensures that the garment allows for unrestricted movement and comfort during daily activities, enhancing its practical usability and wearer satisfaction.

Thirdly, testing closures such as zippers and buttons for functionality and durability under stress conditions is essential. Assessing how well these closures withstand repeated use and stress, ensures they remain reliable and secure throughout the garment's lifespan. This evaluation helps identify potential weak points in design or construction that could affect performance.

Fourthly, performing washing and drying cycles is integral to assessing garment stability and shrinkage. We evaluate how the fabric responds to laundering, including its colorfastness, shrinkage potential, and overall durability after exposure to washing and drying processes. This test ensures that the garment maintains its quality and fit, even after repeated laundering.

Lastly, evaluating the garment's resistance to wrinkles and its ease of ironing provides insights into its practical maintenance requirements. We assess how well the fabric resists wrinkles during wear and how easy it is to restore a smooth appearance through ironing or steaming. This evaluation helps determine the garment's suitability for maintaining a polished look with minimal effort.

Conducting a functional test evaluation focused on performance assessment involves comprehensive testing across elasticity, movement, closures, laundering effects, and wrinkle resistance. By rigorously evaluating these factors, we ensure that each garment meets high standards of durability, functionality, and ease of maintenance, thereby enhancing its overall performance and longevity. This commitment to performance assessment underscores our dedication to delivering garments that not only fit well but also perform reliably under various conditions, meeting the needs and expectations of our customers.

DURABILITY TESTING ASSESSMENT

Performing a Durability Test Assessment on fabric involves meticulous evaluation of several key attributes to ensure its quality and longevity. Fabric strength, seam durability, and colorfastness are critical factors assessed through rigorous testing methodologies.

Fabric strength is evaluated using advanced tensile testing machines that measure both the fabric's strength and elongation at break. This test subjects the fabric to increasing tension until it reaches its breaking point, providing insights into its tensile properties and overall durability. Additionally, resistance to abrasion is assessed through specialized equipment that simulates wear and tear scenarios, gauging the fabric's ability to withstand repeated friction and surface abrasion. Pilling resistance, another crucial aspect, is tested using pilling testers to determine how well the fabric resists the formation of pills, maintaining its smooth surface over time.

Seam strength is examined by applying stress to seams to measure their resistance under tension. This involves checking for any signs of thread popping or loosening, which can compromise the garment's structural integrity. Moreover, the seam's resistance to fraying and unraveling is evaluated, ensuring that it maintains its strength even under challenging conditions. Post-washing tests are conducted to assess the seam's ability to retain its integrity and durability after exposure to laundering processes. Reinforcement in high-stress areas, such as underarm seams, is also scrutinized to ensure optimal performance in areas prone to strain.

Colorfastness tests are conducted to evaluate how well the fabric retains its color over time and through various conditions. Washing tests assess color retention after multiple wash cycles, ensuring the fabric maintains its original hue without fading or discoloration. Light exposure tests simulate sunlight exposure to measure colorfastness against UV radiation, preventing undesirable color changes due to prolonged sun exposure. Furthermore, tests for color transfer assess the fabric's resistance to staining other materials upon contact, while evaluations of resistance to perspiration and water exposure ensure the fabric's color remains vibrant and consistent under different environmental factors.

Conducting comprehensive durability tests on fabric involves a systematic approach to assess fabric strength, seam integrity, and colorfastness. These tests utilize specialized equipment and methodologies to ensure that fabrics meet rigorous quality standards for durability and performance. By evaluating these critical attributes, manufacturers and consumers alike can be assured of the fabric's reliability and longevity in various applications and conditions.

VERIFICATION OF COMPLIANCE AND STANDARDS

In the apparel industry, ensuring compliance with labeling requirements and safety standards is crucial to protect consumers and maintain the integrity of the products. This comprehensive process involves verifying the accuracy and completeness of label information, as well as conducting thorough safety tests to meet regulatory guidelines.

Labeling requirements are a critical aspect of this verification process. Labels must accurately reflect the fiber composition, care instructions, and the country of manufacture, helping consumers make informed purchasing decisions and properly maintain their clothing. Additionally, labels must comply with regional and international regulations in the country of export and the region of one's retail presence.

Depending on the market, labels may need to include additional details, such as size and the Registered Identification Number (RN). Ensuring the presence of all required information enhances transparency and traceability. Furthermore, the label information should be clear, legible, and easy for consumers to understand, promoting effective communication. Finally, labels must be securely attached and able to withstand the rigors of washing, wear, and tear, maintaining the integrity of the label information throughout the product's lifecycle.

Safety standards are another critical aspect of the verification process. Garments must undergo flammability testing to ensure compliance with safety regulations, such as the Consumer Product Safety Commission (CPSC) guidelines or the relevant standards in other regions. Products are also tested for the presence of harmful chemicals and substances to safeguard consumer health and well-being.

The garment's construction is assessed to prevent potential choking hazards, particularly in children's clothing. Specialized clothing, such as high-visibility workwear, must meet specific regulations to ensure the intended level of protection. All safety tests and certifications are thoroughly documented to demonstrate regulatory compliance and provide a comprehensive record for the product.

By meticulously verifying labeling requirements and safety standards, manufacturers and retailers can ensure that their apparel products meet the necessary legal and safety guidelines, ultimately building consumer trust and protecting the well-being of their customers.

FEEDBACK AND ADJUSTMENTS

Gathering internal and external feedback on evaluated garment samples is a crucial step in the design and production process, ensuring that the final product meets high standards of quality, fit, and customer satisfaction. This process involves systematic collection and analysis of input from various stakeholders, both within the organization and from the target market.

Firstly, internal feedback is gathered from design, production, and quality control teams who closely examine the garment sample. Review meetings are held to discuss observations and suggestions in detail, allowing each team to provide insights based on their expertise. Feedback is documented systematically, ensuring all comments and recommendations are easily accessible for reference and action. This documentation is crucial for tracking changes and ensuring all feedback is addressed. Common issues are identified and prioritized for resolution, ensuring that the most critical problems are addressed first.

External feedback is equally important and involves gathering firsthand impressions from the target customers. Organizing focus groups allows for in-depth discussions and immediate feedback on the garment. Additionally, samples can be distributed to selected customers or influencers for wear testing, providing real-world data on fit, comfort, and overall satisfaction. Detailed feedback is collected and analyzed for patterns and recurring themes, which help validate internal assessments. This external feedback is invaluable as it provides a broader perspective and highlights areas that might have been overlooked internally, especially concerning products that are "core" to the business and whose presence will be more significant than the seasonal styles that change every season.

Based on the collected feedback, specific design and technical recommendations are made. Design changes might include altering necklines, hemlines, or adjusting dart placements to improve fit and aesthetics. If the original fabric does not meet expectations, material substitutions may be proposed. Feedback on embellishments or trims can lead to updates that enhance the garment's appeal and functionality. All recommended changes are documented for approval, ensuring that any modifications are well considered and agreed upon before implementation.

Technical recommendations focus on improving the garment's durability and manufacturing quality. Suggestions might include altering seam allowances or construction techniques to enhance durability or changing stitching methods to improve strength. Adjustments to manufacturing processes can help achieve better quality consistency, while identifying areas that need additional reinforcement, such as stress points, ensure the garment can withstand wear and tear. Collaborating with production teams to implement these technical improvements effectively is essential for translating feedback into tangible enhancements in the final product.

Importantly, the process of gathering and analyzing internal and external feedback on garment samples, coupled with targeted design and technical recommendations, is essential for developing high-quality, customer-satisfying products. This collaborative and systematic approach ensures that the final garments meet both aesthetic and functional standards, ultimately leading to a successful product launch.

FINAL APPROVAL AND DOCUMENTATION

A final review meeting for garment sample evaluations is a critical step in ensuring the readiness of a product for mass production. This meeting involves a cross-functional team including representatives from design, production, marketing, and quality assurance. During the meeting, all feedback, testing results, and recommended adjustments are reviewed in detail. This collaborative approach ensures that any potential issues are addressed comprehensively, with each department providing insights on how adjustments might impact production timelines and costs. The goal is to make informed decisions on any outstanding issues or changes, ensuring that the final product meets the desired standards.

The outcome of the review meeting is thoroughly documented. This includes noting all decisions made, adjustments agreed upon, and next steps to be taken. Final approval from key stakeholders, such as designers and brand managers, is essential to move forward. It is crucial to ensure that all changes have been implemented and tested in the final sample. Once the final sample is approved, it is signed off as the standard for mass production. Communication of this approval to the production teams is vital to initiate mass manufacturing. Monitoring initial production runs is also necessary to ensure consistency with the approved sample, thus maintaining quality and reducing the risk of defects.

Updating the technical pack is a crucial part of this process. The tech pack should be revised to include finalized measurements, materials, and construction details. Detailed notes on any changes made during the sample evaluation process must be added to ensure clarity. This documentation should be clear and accessible to the production teams, with visual aids such as diagrams or photographs to clarify specifications. Keeping a record of all versions of the tech pack is important for reference and traceability, aiding in future evaluations and potential troubleshooting.

Additionally, developing a comprehensive quality control plan based on the sample evaluation findings is essential. This plan should define quality standards and acceptable tolerances for mass production, outline inspection procedures and checkpoints throughout the production process, and ensure quality control personnel are trained on the specific requirements of the garment. Establishing a system for ongoing monitoring and feedback is crucial for continuous improvement, ensuring that the final product consistently meets the high standards set during the review meeting. This structured approach helps in maintaining product quality and customer satisfaction.

CHAPTER 7

CHECK THAT OUT – QUALITY CONTROL AND QUALITY ASSURANCE

QA VS QC

In the apparel industry, quality control (QC) and quality assurance (QA) are two critical components that ensure the final products meet the desired standards and customer expectations. Although they are often used interchangeably, they refer to distinct processes. Quality control is primarily focused on identifying defects in the finished products. It involves a series of inspections and tests at various stages of production to detect and rectify any issues that could compromise the quality of the garments. For instance, quality control inspectors might check for inconsistencies in stitching, fabric flaws, or deviations from the design specifications. This reactive approach aims to catch defects before the products reach the consumer, ensuring that only items meeting the set quality standards are shipped out.

On the other hand, quality assurance is a more holistic and proactive approach that encompasses the entire production process, from the initial design phase to the final product delivery. Quality assurance involves establishing and maintaining a system of procedures and standards to prevent defects from occurring in the first place. This can include implementing standardized processes, conducting regular training for staff, and continuously reviewing and improving production methods. In the apparel industry, QA might involve ensuring that fabrics and materials are sourced from reliable suppliers, setting precise specifications for each garment, and monitoring compliance with these standards throughout the production cycle. The goal of QA is to build quality into the product from the start, reducing the likelihood of defects and enhancing overall efficiency.

A key difference between QC and QA in the apparel industry lies in their timing and focus. Quality control is typically performed at the end of the production line, focusing on the finished products and their compliance with predefined standards. It is essentially a defect detection mechanism, where the emphasis is on identifying and correcting errors after they have occurred. Conversely, quality assurance is integrated into every stage of the production process, emphasizing defect prevention. By focusing on process optimization, staff training, and systematic checks, QA aims to ensure that the production environment consistently produces high-quality garments, thus minimizing the need for extensive QC interventions.

The interplay between quality control and quality assurance is crucial for maintaining high standards in the apparel industry. While quality control acts as the final gatekeeper to catch any issues before products reach the market, quality assurance creates a robust framework that supports consistent quality throughout the design process, during product development, and production cycle. By combining these two approaches, apparel retailers, and apparel manufacturers can ensure that their products not only meet but exceed customer expectations, thereby building a strong reputation for quality and reliability in a highly competitive market. This synergy ultimately leads to reduced costs, fewer returns, and increased customer satisfaction.

RAW MATERIAL INSPECTION

The quality of the final product is significantly influenced by the quality of the raw materials used. High standards in raw material inspection are essential to ensure that only materials that meet specific criteria are utilized in the production process. This is particularly important in industries like textiles and apparel, where the materials directly affect the durability, appearance, and overall performance of the final products. Conducting thorough inspections upon the arrival of raw materials such as fabrics, threads, buttons, and zippers can prevent defects and ensure consistency in the finished goods.

Inspecting raw materials begins with a comprehensive assessment as soon as they are received. Fabrics, for instance, are scrutinized for weight, colorfastness, shrinkage, and tensile strength. These parameters are crucial as they affect the fabric's performance and suitability for its intended use. The fabric's weight impacts its drape and feel, while colorfastness ensures that the color remains stable during washing and wear. Shrinkage tests determine how much the fabric will contract after washing, and tensile strength tests ensure the fabric can withstand stretching and pulling forces.

For threads, buttons, and zippers, similar rigorous checks are performed. Threads are tested for strength and durability to ensure they do not break easily during stitching or wear. Buttons are checked for their attachment strength and resistance to breaking or cracking under pressure. Zippers are tested for smooth operation, durability, and their ability to withstand repeated use without failure. These inspections help in identifying any potential weaknesses or defects in the raw materials, ensuring that only those meeting the required standards proceed to the production phase.

Materials that fail to meet the predefined standards are either rejected outright or returned to the supplier for replacement or refund. This step is crucial to maintain the integrity of the production process and the quality of the final product. Rejecting substandard materials prevents the incorporation of inferior components into the production line, which could compromise the product's quality and performance. By ensuring that all raw materials adhere to high-quality standards, manufacturers can produce reliable and superior products, ultimately leading to greater customer satisfaction and brand reputation.

IN PROCESS OR INLINE INSPECTIONS

Conducting inspections at various stages of the production process is essential for identifying defects early and ensuring the quality of the final product. This practice, known as in-process or inline inspection, allows for continuous monitoring and evaluation, which can catch issues before they escalate. By implementing these inspections, manufacturers can maintain control over production quality, ensuring that each piece meets the required standards and specifications.

In-process inspections typically begin with checking the accuracy of cutting patterns. Precision in cutting is crucial as it determines the fit and appearance of the garment. Any discrepancies at this stage can lead to significant defects that are difficult to correct later. Inspectors verify that the patterns are cut according to the design specifications and that the pieces align perfectly. This step ensures that the foundation of the garment is correct, which is critical for the subsequent assembly stages.

The next focus of in-process inspections is the precision of stitching. Inspectors monitor the stitching for consistency, strength, and adherence to design details. They check for issues such as loose threads, uneven seams, or incorrect stitch types, all of which can affect the garment's durability and appearance. By identifying these issues early, the quality control team can address them immediately, preventing flawed products from continuing through the production line.

Finally, proper assembly of garment components is crucial. During this stage, inspectors ensure that all parts of the garment are correctly assembled according to the design specifications. This includes verifying the correct placement and attachment of buttons, zippers, and other fasteners. Inline quality control teams monitor each step, ensuring that each component fits together perfectly and functions as intended. This proactive approach helps prevent defects from progressing to later stages of production, reducing the need for costly rework and enhancing overall product quality. Through meticulous in-process inspections, manufacturers can maintain high standards, ensuring that the final products meet or exceed customer expectations.

FINAL INSPECTIONS

Once the garments are fully assembled, a thorough inspection of the final products is essential to ensure that they meet the highest quality standards. This final inspection process involves a comprehensive evaluation of the overall garment quality, including critical aspects such as measurements, fit, finishing, and packaging. By conducting this detailed inspection, manufacturers can ensure that each and every defect is identified and corrected before the products reach the customers.

The inspection begins with checking the measurements and fit of the garments. Inspectors verify that the garments conform to the specified dimensions and sizing standards. This step is crucial to ensure that each piece fits as intended and meets the customers' expectations. Any discrepancies in size or fit can lead to customer dissatisfaction and returns, so precision at this stage is vital for maintaining the brand's reputation.

Next, the inspection focuses on the finishing of the garments. Inspectors look for defects such as loose threads, misaligned seams, or incorrect labels. These details, though seemingly minor, significantly impact the overall appearance and quality of the product. Loose threads can lead to unraveling, misaligned seams can affect the garment's structure and aesthetic, and incorrect labels can cause confusion and dissatisfaction among customers. By identifying and correcting these issues, the final inspection ensures that each garment is flawless and ready for market.

Final inspections are typically conducted in batches, with a sample of finished products reviewed to ensure they meet the company's quality standards. This sampling approach allows for efficient quality control while providing a representative overview of the entire production batch. By examining a selection of products, inspectors can detect any recurring issues or patterns of defects that need to be addressed. This method ensures that the overall quality of the batch is up to standard, and any problematic items are flagged and corrected before shipping.

In conclusion, the final inspection is a crucial step in the quality control process, ensuring that the finished garments meet the highest standards of quality and consistency. By thoroughly checking measurements, fit, finishing, and packaging, manufacturers can identify and correct any defects, ensuring that only top-quality products reach the customers. This meticulous process helps maintain the brand's reputation, reduces the likelihood of returns, and enhances customer satisfaction.

STATISTICAL PROCESS CONTROL (SPC)

Implementing statistical methods to monitor and control production quality, known as Statistical Process Control (SPC), significantly enhances the effectiveness of quality control mechanisms. SPC involves using statistical tools and techniques to understand and manage variations in the production process, ensuring that the output consistently meets quality standards. By incorporating SPC, manufacturers can maintain a high level of quality control, minimize defects, and improve overall production efficiency.

One of the key techniques in SPC is the use of control charts. Control charts help monitor the production process by plotting data points over time and identifying any variations that fall outside predefined control limits. These charts make it easy to detect trends, shifts, or any unusual patterns in the process that could indicate potential problems. By continuously tracking these variations, manufacturers can quickly respond to any deviations from the norm, ensuring that corrective actions are taken before defects become widespread.

Another important aspect of SPC is the implementation of sampling plans. Sampling plans involve selecting a representative sample of products from a production batch to be inspected and analyzed. This method provides a practical and efficient way to monitor production quality without having to inspect every single item. By analyzing the sampled data, manufacturers can make informed decisions about the entire batch, identifying any quality issues and determining whether further inspection or corrective actions are necessary.

Process capability analysis is also a crucial part of SPC. This technique assesses the ability of a production process to produce items within specified tolerance limits consistently. By analyzing process capability, manufacturers can determine whether their processes are stable and capable of meeting quality standards. If the analysis reveals that the process is not capable, adjustments can be made to improve it. This proactive approach helps in maintaining a high level of quality control and reduces the likelihood of defects.

In conclusion, Statistical Process Control (SPC) is a powerful tool for monitoring and controlling production quality. By utilizing techniques such as control charts, sampling plans, and process capability analysis, manufacturers can understand variations in the production process and maintain consistency. Analyzing data from these methods enables the identification of trends and recurring issues, allowing for data-driven decisions to improve quality. Through SPC, manufacturers can achieve greater efficiency, reduce defects, and ensure that their products meet the highest quality standards.

ACCEPTABLE QUALITY LEVEL (AQL)

In the apparel industry, conducting an inspection based on Acceptable Quality Level (AQL) involves a systematic process designed to assess product quality and ensure that it meets specified standards. The AQL system is a statistical method used to determine the maximum number of defective items considered acceptable in a particular sample size. AQL is a common standard that represents a middle ground between strict and lenient quality control. Here's a step-by-step overview of the procedure:

Preparation for inspection is essential. The inspector gathers all necessary documentation, including purchase orders, specifications, and quality standards. These documents outline the criteria that the garments must meet. The inspector also prepares the inspection tools, such as measurement tapes, fabric weight scales, and color swatches. The inspection area should be well-lit and clean to facilitate accurate assessment. Before starting, the inspector verifies that the production lot is complete and ready for inspection, ensuring no further work is being done on the garments.

The inspector determines the sample size based on the total quantity of garments in the lot using the AQL tables. For instance, if the order quantity falls between 501 to 1200 pieces, the inspector will select 80 garments to inspect. The sample size and acceptance criteria (number of allowable defects) are determined by the AQL level's classified by the nature of defects. The garments are selected randomly to ensure an unbiased inspection. This random selection is crucial as it gives a representative overview of the entire production lot's quality.

During the inspection phase, the inspector examines each selected garment thoroughly. The inspection covers various aspects, including measurements, workmanship, fabric quality, color consistency, and overall appearance. Specific checkpoints might include checking for loose threads, broken stitches, stains, color variations, and incorrect sizing. The inspector uses the defect classification system to categorize any issues found. Defects are typically classified as critical, major, or minor. In AQL 2.5, the acceptance criteria allow a maximum of 5 major defects, and AQL 4.0 being a reference for minor defects allow a maximum of 7 defects, but the tolerance for critical defects is zero. The classification of defects is explained clearly in the following sub-chapter.

Finally, the evaluation and reporting stage concludes the inspection process. The inspector compares the number of defects found against the AQL acceptance criteria. If the number of defects is within the acceptable range, the lot passes the inspection. If it exceeds the allowable defects, the lot fails. The inspector documents all findings in a detailed report, highlighting any defects and their classifications. This report is shared with the manufacturer and the client. If the lot fails, the manufacturer must address the issues and may need to rework the garments before a re-inspection is scheduled. This systematic approach ensures that only garments meeting the specified quality standards are approved, maintaining the integrity and reputation of the brand.

CLASSIFICATION OF DEFECTS

In the apparel industry, Acceptable Quality Level (AQL) classifies defects into three main categories: Minor, Major and Critical. These classifications help ensure quality control by identifying the severity of defects and determining the necessary actions to address them. Following is a detailed explanation of each class:

Minor Defects

Minor defects are less severe issues that do not significantly affect the garment's usability or appearance. These defects are often less noticeable and may not be perceived by the customer. They typically do not lead to returns but may slightly reduce the perceived quality of the item. Examples include:

- Slight color variations or shading differences
- Small, unobtrusive stains or marks
- Minor misalignment of trims or buttons

- Slight puckering or loose threads that can be easily fixed

- Inconsistent stitching that does not affect the garment's durability

Major Defects

Major defects are significant issues that affect the usability, appearance, or longevity of the apparel item. These defects are likely to be noticed by the customer and can lead to dissatisfaction or returns. Major defects do not necessarily render the garment unusable, but they significantly detract from its quality. Examples include:

- Noticeable fabric flaws (e.g., cuts or holes)

- Incorrect measurements (e.g., sleeves that are too short or long)

- Poor seam construction leading to weak or easily torn seams

- Misaligned patterns or prints

- Incorrect labeling or sizing

Critical Defects

Critical defects are the most severe type of defects that can render a garment unusable or unsafe. These defects pose a significant risk to the consumer and can lead to serious consequences, such as injury. Critical defects require immediate attention and typically result in the garment being rejected or recalled. Examples include:

- Sharp objects or foreign materials embedded in the garment (e.g., broken needles)

- Loose components that can cause choking hazards (e.g., buttons or decorative elements)

- Extremely poor construction that compromises the garment's integrity

- Toxic or harmful substances used in the fabric or accessories

- Structural issues that make the garment non-wearable (e.g., completely mismatched parts or missing essential components)

Understanding these defect classifications helps manufacturers and quality control teams prioritize their inspection processes, address issues appropriately, and maintain high standards of quality in the apparel industry.

EMBEDDING QUALITY ASSURANCE IN PRODUCT DEVELOPMENT OPERATIONS

Embedding Quality Assurance (QA) into the product development process in the apparel industry begins at the design phase. Here, QA ensures that designs are not only aesthetically pleasing but also manufacturable with high quality. This involves setting clear, detailed specifications for fabrics, trims, and construction techniques. By collaborating with designers, QA teams can foresee potential production issues and suggest modifications early, preventing costly errors later. Establishing precise guidelines and standards at this stage ensures that everyone involved in production understands the quality expectations.

During the sourcing phase, QA plays a critical role in selecting reliable suppliers and materials that meet predetermined quality standards. This includes evaluating suppliers' capabilities and conducting audits to ensure they comply with industry standards and ethical practices. Regular assessments and building strong relationships with suppliers help in maintaining consistent material quality. Additionally, implementing a robust material testing protocol ensures that fabrics and other components meet specific requirements before entering the production line, reducing the risk of defects and ensuring product durability and performance.

In the production phase, QA involves continuous monitoring and systematic checks to maintain quality throughout the manufacturing process. This includes setting up in-line inspection points where QA inspectors review the product at various stages of assembly. These inspections help identify and correct issues promptly, ensuring that problems do not escalate to later stages. Implementing standard operating procedures (SOPs) for each production step ensures consistency and reduces variability, which is crucial for maintaining high quality across large batches of garments.

Finally, QA extends to the post-production phase, where the focus is on evaluating the final product and incorporating feedback for continuous improvement. This involves thorough final inspections to ensure the finished garments meet all quality criteria. Additionally, collecting and analyzing feedback from customers and retailers helps identify recurring issues and areas for enhancement. By fostering a culture of continuous improvement and responsiveness to feedback, QA ensures that the lessons learned are applied to future product development cycles, continuously elevating the quality of apparel produced.

CHAPTER 8

SURGICAL INTERVENTION – TESTING PARAMETERS

Classified as "Chemical testing, physical testing, and analytical testing," testing textiles and apparel is crucial in the fashion industry to ensure quality, safety, and compliance with regulatory standards.

Chemical tests in the apparel industry involve analyzing the chemical composition and properties of textiles and garments. These tests ensure that fabrics are free from harmful substances, such as formaldehyde, lead, and azo dyes. They also evaluate colorfastness, pH levels, and chemical resistance. Common methods include gas chromatography, spectrophotometry, and titration. The goal is to ensure the safety, compliance with regulations, and longevity of the garments, ensuring they do not cause skin irritation or health issues for consumers.

Physical tests assess the mechanical and physical properties of textiles and garments, such as strength, durability, and comfort. These tests include tensile strength, abrasion resistance, pilling, dimensional stability, and seam slippage. Instruments like tensile testers, Martindale abrasion testers, and pilling boxes are used. The purpose is to ensure the product can withstand wear and tear, maintain its appearance and functionality after use and washing, and meet quality standards.

Analytical tests in the apparel industry involve precise measurements and evaluations of various material properties through advanced techniques and instruments. These tests include both chemical and physical analysis, but with a focus on detailed quantification and characterization. Examples include fiber content analysis, moisture regain, and thermal properties. Techniques like chromatography, spectroscopy, and microscopy are commonly used. The aim is to gain a deeper understanding of the material's composition, structure, and behavior, supporting product development, quality control, and compliance with industry standards.

SOME FREQUENTLY CONDUCTED CHEMICAL TESTS

PH VALUE TESTING

pH Value Testing in the apparel industry serves to assess the acidity or alkalinity of fabrics and garments, crucial for both manufacturing processes and consumer safety.

Objective – The purpose of pH testing is twofold: first, to ensure that textiles are compatible with human skin, minimizing the risk of irritation or allergic reactions; second, to optimize dyeing processes, as pH affects the adherence and color intensity of dyes on fabrics.

Method – The method involves soaking a fabric sample in water and measuring the pH of the resulting solution using a pH meter or indicator strips. The pH scale, ranging from 0 to 14, categorizes solutions as acidic (0–7), neutral (7), or alkaline (7–14). For outerwear, the acceptable pH range is 4 to 9, while for garments in direct contact with the skin, such as lingerie and undergarments, the range is stricter at 4 to 7.5. This straightforward test delivers quick results, enabling manufacturers to adjust processing conditions to achieve safe and acceptable pH levels.

Importance – the importance of pH testing lies in its role in ensuring product safety and quality. Fabrics with improper pH levels can cause discomfort or skin reactions in consumers, leading to dissatisfaction or health concerns. Moreover, maintaining the correct pH during manufacturing ensures consistent dye uptake and colorfastness, enhancing the aesthetic appeal and durability of garments. Compliance with pH standards is essential for meeting regulatory requirements and consumer expectations for high-quality apparel that is both comfortable and safe to wear.

FORMALDEHYDE CONTENT

Formaldehyde testing in the apparel industry aims to measure the presence and quantity of formaldehyde, a chemical known to cause skin irritation and allergic reactions.

Objective–The primary purpose is to ensure that textiles and garments meet safety standards by limiting formaldehyde levels to prevent adverse health effects in consumers.

Method–The test typically involves extracting formaldehyde from the fabric using a water extraction method. The extracted formaldehyde is then analyzed using spectrophotometric techniques or other analytical methods to quantify its concentration.

Importance–Controlling formaldehyde content is crucial for compliance with international regulations such as REACH and Oeko-Tex standards, which set limits on formaldehyde emissions from textiles. By conducting formaldehyde testing, manufacturers can ensure that their products are safe for consumer use, minimizing the risk of skin irritation and allergic reactions.

AZO DYE TESTING

Azo dye testing detects the presence of azo dyes that can release carcinogenic amines when they come into contact with sweat or saliva.

Objective – The objective is to ensure that textiles are free from harmful azo dyes, protecting consumer health.

Method – The test involves extracting the dyes from the fabric and analyzing them using gas chromatography or high-performance liquid chromatography (HPLC) to detect the presence of specific amines.

Importance – Compliance with regulations such as the European Regulation (EC) No 1907/2006 (REACH) and the Oeko-Tex Standard 100 ensures that textiles do not contain azo dyes that could pose health risks. Azo dye testing helps manufacturers verify the safety of their products and assure consumers that their garments are free from harmful substances.

COLORFASTNESS TESTING

Colorfastness testing evaluates how well a fabric retains its color when exposed to various conditions such as washing, light, and rubbing.

Objective – The objective is to ensure that textiles maintain their aesthetic appeal and do not transfer color onto other surfaces during use.

Method – Different tests assess colorfastness to washing, light, rubbing, perspiration, and other factors using standardized procedures. Spectrophotometric analysis quantifies color change.

Importance–Ensuring colorfastness is crucial for maintaining garment quality and customer satisfaction. Garments that retain their color over time enhance brand reputation and consumer trust. Colorfastness testing helps manufacturers identify suitable dyes and finishes to achieve durable and vibrant colors while meeting performance expectations.

CHLORINATED PHENOLS

Testing for chlorinated phenols in textiles identifies harmful substances used in textile processing, such as bleaching and finishing agents.

Objective–The objective is to ensure that textiles do not contain chlorinated phenols that can harm human health and the environment.

Method–Analysis involves extracting and quantifying chlorinated phenols using techniques like gas chromatography coupled with mass spectrometry (GC-MS).

Importance–Compliance with regulations such as REACH ensures that textiles are free from hazardous chemicals. Testing for chlorinated phenols helps manufacturers and brands uphold sustainability and safety standards, ensuring consumer protection and environmental responsibility in textile production.

SOME FREQUENTLY CONDUCTED PHYSICAL TESTS

TENSILE STRENGTH

Tensile strength testing evaluates the maximum force a fabric can withstand before breaking or deforming.

Objective – The objective is to assess durability and ensure fabrics can withstand the stresses of wear and laundering without tearing.

Method – Fabric samples are stretched using a tensile testing machine until they rupture. The force at breaking point is recorded to quantify tensile strength.

Importance – Tensile strength informs manufacturers about fabric durability, guiding material selection and garment design. It ensures garments withstand daily wear and stress, meeting consumer expectations for longevity and performance.

TEAR STRENGTH

Tear strength testing measures a fabric's resistance to tearing under tension, evaluating its ability to withstand accidental pulls or stress.

Objective – The objective is to assess durability and prevent premature tearing during use.

Method – Fabric samples are subjected to tension until they tear, with the force required recorded using an Elmendorf or similar tester.

Importance – Tear strength data guides material selection and product design, ensuring garments withstand wear and tear. It enhances garment durability, prolonging product life and customer satisfaction.

ABRASION RESISTANCE

Abrasion resistance testing assesses how well a fabric withstands rubbing and friction.

Objective – The purpose is to evaluate durability and ensure fabrics maintain their appearance over time.

Method – Fabric samples are rubbed against an abrasive surface using a Martindale or Taber tester. The number of cycles until visible wear or yarn breakage occurs is recorded.

Importance – Abrasion resistance data informs material choices for garments subjected to friction, such as work wear or upholstery. It ensures fabrics retain their aesthetic and functional properties, enhancing product quality and longevity.

PILLING RESISTANCE

Pilling resistance testing evaluates a fabric's tendency to form pills or fuzz balls during wear.

Objective – The objective is to maintain garment's appearance and quality.

Method – Fabric samples are subjected to rubbing or abrasion using a pilling tester. The formation of pills is assessed visually or quantitatively.

Importance – Pilling resistance data helps manufacturers select fabrics that maintain a smooth appearance over time. It ensures garments look newer for longer, enhancing customer satisfaction and brand reputation.

DIMENSIONAL STABILITY

Dimensional stability testing measures how well a fabric retains its size and shape after laundering or exposure to moisture.

Objective – The purpose is to ensure garments fit consistently and maintain their intended dimensions.

Method – Fabric samples are washed or conditioned according to standard procedures, and dimensional changes are measured using a ruler or dimensional stability tester.

Importance – Dimensional stability data guides material selection and garment construction, preventing shrinkage or distortion. It ensures garments maintain their fit and shape, enhancing comfort and customer satisfaction.

MOISTURE MANAGEMENT

Moisture management testing assesses how well a fabric absorbs, transports, and evaporates moisture.

Objective–The purpose is to enhance comfort and performance in various climates.

Method–Fabric samples are exposed to moisture, and properties such as absorption rate, wicking ability, and drying time are measured.

Importance–Moisture management data helps manufacturers design fabrics that keep wearers dry and comfortable. It ensures garments perform well during physical activities or in humid conditions, meeting consumer expectations for functionality.

STATIC ELECTRICITY

Static electricity testing evaluates a fabric's tendency to generate or hold static charges.

Objective–The objective is to ensure comfort and prevent static-related discomfort during wear.

Method–Fabric samples are tested for static build-up using a static meter or by rubbing against other materials to observe charge generation.

Importance–Static electricity data guides material selection for garments, especially in synthetic fabrics.

It ensures garments are comfortable to wear and do not cling or generate static, enhancing user experience and satisfaction.

SOME FREQUENTLY CONDUCTED ANALYTICAL TESTS

FIBER CONTENT ANALYSIS

Fiber content analysis determines and measures the types and proportions of fibers in a textile sample. While the testing involves the use of chemicals, its primary purpose is to analyze the percentages and composition of the yarns that make up the fabric.

Objective – The objective is to ensure accurate labeling and compliance with regulatory standards regarding fiber composition.

Method – Techniques such as microscopy and chemical dissolution are used to distinguish between natural and synthetic fibers. Results are crucial for verifying product specifications and ensuring consistency in manufacturing.

Importance – Fiber content analysis is essential for quality control and consumer protection. It helps manufacturers meet legal requirements for textile labeling and ensures products deliver expected performance and characteristics.

DIMENSIONAL STABILITY ANALYSIS

Dimensional stability analysis measures changes in fabric dimensions after laundering or exposure to moisture.

Objective–The purpose is to ensure garments maintain their size and shape, meeting consumer expectations for fit and comfort.

Method–Fabric samples are washed or conditioned according to standardized procedures, and dimensional changes are measured using precision instruments.

Importance–Dimensional stability testing guides material selection and production processes to prevent shrinkage or distortion. It ensures garments retain their intended dimensions throughout their lifecycle, enhancing wearability and durability.

PERFORMANCE TESTING

Performance testing assesses specific functional properties of textiles, such as moisture management, breathability, and thermal insulation.

Objective–The purpose is to ensure garments perform well under intended conditions and meet consumer needs for comfort and functionality.

Method – Tests use specialized equipment like differential scanning calorimetry (DSC) or moisture regain testers to evaluate performance characteristics.

Importance – Performance testing helps manufacturers develop textiles that meet market demands for performance and comfort. It ensures garments perform effectively in diverse environments, enhancing customer satisfaction and brand reputation.

CHAPTER 9

KEEPING FASHION MOVING – LOGISTICS & SUPPLY CHAIN

INVENTORY MANAGEMENT

Efficient inventory management in the fashion industry depends on automated systems that monitor stock levels in real-time. Technologies such as RFID (Radio Frequency Identification) and barcode scanning facilitate the tracking of inventory, providing precise stock counts. Demand forecasting, enhanced by AI and historical data, anticipates future requirements, while stock optimization aligns expenses with customer demand. ABC analysis (product categorization in inventory management) prioritizes high-value items for more effective management.

Frequent cycle counting guarantees inventory accuracy without the need for complete audits, while routine checks assist in identifying and rectifying inconsistencies. Collaborating with suppliers to manage lead times ensures timely restocking, which helps to avoid shortages. Synchronizing inventory across various sales platforms ensures product accessibility, enhancing customer satisfaction.

Maintaining safety stock provides a cushion against unforeseen demand or supply interruptions. A robust system not only oversees inventory but also forecasts demand, balances stock levels, and synchronizes supplier schedules. These methods enable fashion retailers to prevent overstocking while quickly processing customer orders. By leveraging real-time tracking, regular cycle counts, and demand forecasting, businesses can ensure precise inventory management and improve the shopping experience, guaranteeing that products are readily available across all channels.

SUPPLIER COORDINATION

Effective collaboration with suppliers is essential for fashion brands to achieve timely, quality-driven, and cost-effective production. Supplier scorecards facilitate the assessment of performance in terms of quality, dependability, and expenses. Frequent communication, such as regular meetings, helps keep all parties informed and aligned, while well-articulated contracts eliminate ambiguity by specifying expectations.

Expanding the supplier network mitigates risks and fosters a resilient supply chain. Digital collaboration tools enable seamless communication and document sharing, streamlining processes. Conducting quality checks at supplier facilities prior to shipping ensures compliance with standards, and providing training assists suppliers in comprehending and upholding brand expectations.

Planning orders in advance synchronizes with suppliers' production timelines, avoiding potential delays. Collaborative improvement initiatives promote innovation and provide mutual benefits. Acknowledging cultural differences enhances relationships, leading to smoother operations.

Through the use of scorecards, straightforward contracts, digital tools, and training, fashion brands can establish a robust supplier network that consistently meets quality and timing benchmarks. This coordinated strategy cultivates an efficient supply chain that reliably delivers high-quality products to customers on schedule and within budget.

WAREHOUSING

Strategic storage is essential for fashion companies, starting with selecting warehouse locations close to major markets and transport routes. Using Warehouse Management Systems (WMS) improves processes and boosts efficiency, while optimizing warehouse layouts maximizes space and streamlines workflow. Cross-docking, which minimizes storage time by quickly transferring items, speeds up delivery—vital for fast-moving fashion goods.

Climate control solutions ensure delicate items are stored in optimal conditions, and strong security measures prevent theft and damage. Automated picking and sorting systems reduce manual work and errors, increasing overall efficiency. Specialized areas handle returns, making reverse logistics faster and ensuring quick restocking.

Effective scheduling of manpower allotment boosts productivity and reduces costs. Eco-friendly practices, like energy-efficient lighting and recycling, support sustainability goals. Strategic warehousing combines location, layout, and advanced technology, while climate control and security safeguard valuable inventory.

Automation and dedicated returns processes ensure smooth operations and prompt replenishment. By maximizing efficiency and adopting sustainable practices, fashion companies can create a warehouse system that balances efficiency, cost savings, and environmental care, ultimately enhancing customer satisfaction.

PACKAGING

Product packaging is essential for balancing protection, branding, and sustainability. It should ensure garments are secure during shipping and represent the brand's identity, creating a memorable experience for customers. Protective materials guarantee that items arrive without damage, while eco-friendly alternatives, such as recyclable materials, cater to environmentally conscious consumers.

Streamlining packaging dimensions helps lower shipping expenses and minimizes material waste. Custom inserts offer additional protection for specific products, ensuring they reach customers in perfect condition, while clear labeling simplifies handling and reduces logistical mistakes. Quality packaging must align with brand expectations while adhering to budget constraints.

Utilizing reusable packaging and following regulations further enhances sustainability efforts and ensures compliance. Eye-catching and practical packaging improves the unboxing experience, delivering added value to customers. By selecting materials that provide both protection and sustainability, fashion brands can send products in top condition while lessening their ecological footprint. Comprehensively designed packaging enhances customer satisfaction, promotes sustainability, and fosters a positive experience that aligns with the brand's mission.

TRANSPORTATION MANAGEMENT

Managing logistics in the fashion industry involves selecting carriers based on expense, dependability, and delivery speed to find a balance between urgency and costs. Choosing the appropriate mode—whether it be air, sea, rail, or road—ensures shipments are both timely and economical. Establishing strong relationships with carriers enhances reliability and service quality, resulting in smoother delivery processes.

Utilizing route optimization tools increases efficiency by pinpointing the most affordable routes. Freight consolidation brings together multiple shipments, lowering overall logistics expenses. Real-time tracking keeps clients updated, boosting satisfaction and trust levels.

Anticipating possible delays can help alleviate disruptions. Conducting regular freight audits can uncover billing errors and identify cost-saving opportunities, streamlining operations. Embracing environmentally friendly solutions, such as electric or hybrid transportation, aligns with sustainability objectives by decreasing emissions.

Successful transportation management achieves a balance among cost, speed, and reliability, guaranteeing deliveries are timely and meet customer expectations. Simplifying customs procedures is also crucial in preventing delays, which is especially vital for fashion brands looking to expand their global presence.

CUSTOMS AND COMPLIANCE

It is crucial to handle customs and compliance effectively to prevent expensive mistakes and delays. Ensuring proper documentation and precise tariff classification guarantees the appropriate duties and taxes are applied, helping to avoid unforeseen costs. Utilizing trade agreements can also decrease customs expenses, offering financial advantages. Educating employees on international trade regulations is vital for maintaining smooth and compliant operations.

Collaborating with experienced customs brokers can accelerate customs clearance, minimizing delays. Duty drawback programs enable businesses to recover duties paid on exported products, enhancing cost efficiency. Keeping abreast of changes in trade regulations and obtaining import permits in advance can avert legal complications and ensure adherence to compliance.

Products must adhere to labeling requirements for the countries they are being sent to, thus implementing risk management strategies helps lessen disruptions related to customs. Successful management of customs and compliance hinges on thorough documentation, accurate classification, and the utilization of trade agreements. Knowledgeable employees and partnerships with customs brokers help streamline processes, while duty drawback programs help lower costs.

Remaining informed about regulations and acquiring essential licenses ahead of time ensures international shipments proceed smoothly. By guaranteeing compliance with labeling standards and effectively managing risks, fashion businesses can facilitate the seamless movement of their products across borders.

THE HOME RUN

Last-mile delivery of fashion products seeks to accommodate a variety of customer preferences by providing multiple delivery alternatives. Real-time tracking allows customers to stay updated on the progress of their orders, while collaborations with local carriers expedite delivery, enhancing overall satisfaction. Offering customers the option to choose their preferred delivery time slots further improves their experience.

Implementing secure delivery methods helps mitigate theft and loss, safeguarding inventory. Keeping customers informed about the delivery status fosters trust, while simple and affordable return processes boost customer loyalty. Optimizing delivery costs guarantees efficiency without compromising the quality of service.

Utilizing eco-friendly vehicles or techniques reduces the ecological footprint of last-mile delivery. Analyzing data reveals opportunities for enhancements, improving delivery effectiveness. By integrating diverse delivery options, real-time notifications, and local partnerships, efficient last-mile delivery cultivates both speed and reliability.

Secure delivery methods, open communication, and convenient return procedures foster customer trust and satisfaction. Cost-effectiveness and sustainable practices are in line with business objectives and environmental stewardship, while insights gained from data analysis encourage ongoing improvement in the last-mile delivery process.

RETURNS MANAGEMENT

Efficient returns management in the fashion industry begins with a straightforward, customer-centric return policy. An effective reverse logistics system allows for rapid processing of returns, with inspected items evaluated for resale potential to minimize waste. Swiftly restocking returned items that can be resold minimizes inventory losses and accommodates customer demand.

Prompt processing of refunds enhances customer satisfaction and fosters repeat purchases. Providing free or inexpensive return shipping options further improves the customer experience. Examining return data can help pinpoint frequent problems, informing product enhancements, while feedback from returns contributes to the development of superior products and services.

Refurbishing and reselling items that cannot be offered as new helps lower waste and recoup costs. Environmentally-responsible disposal of unsold returns aligns with sustainability initiatives. Successful returns management brings together clear policies, streamlined logistics, and comprehensive inspections to maximize resale value and reduce waste.

Timely refunds and convenient return shipping options boost customer satisfaction, while insights from data and feedback drive product innovation. The refurbishing process and responsible disposal practices lessen environmental impacts, supporting sustainability objectives.

CHAPTER 10

FUNCTIONAL FRAMEWORK – STRUCTURING DEPARTMENTS

PRODUCT DEVELOPMENT DEPARTMENT

The product development department comprises teams directly engaged in creating products, including Design, Buying, Technical, and Quality Assurance. Quality Assurance (QA) plays a crucial role at a corporate level by establishing operational standards. QA ensures that quality permeates every aspect of the product development department. This involves documenting procedures comprehensively for team-wide acknowledgment, understanding, and strict adherence. Standard Operating Procedures (SOPs) and Product Quality Standards are established to benchmark and align expectations with industry and corporate norms. Additionally, QA establishes clear formats for precise internal and external communications, minimizing ambiguity.

While this summary provides a brief overview, the exhaustive work of each team cannot be fully encapsulated here. Each of the four core teams within the Product Development Department—Design, Buying, Technical, and Quality—operates through extensive and diligent efforts, contributing significantly to the department's overall function.

DESIGN DEPARTMENT

The Fashion Design Department is the creative engine behind every apparel and accessory collection, where market trends and consumer needs come to life. At its core, this team transforms ideas into innovative, stylish products, starting with deep market research, design brainstorming, and prototype development. Close collaboration with marketing and production ensures designs are both feasible and aligned with the brand's vision.

Key skills within the team include creativity, technical drawing, and an understanding of textiles and garment construction. Designers must have an eye for detail, a strong sense of color, and be proficient in tools like Adobe Illustrator and CAD. However, success also relies on effective communication and teamwork to ensure seamless transitions from concept to creation.

Diverse knowledge enhances the team's ability to stay ahead of the curve. Familiarity with sustainable fashion, digital design, and trend forecasting helps create relevant, forward-thinking collections. Understanding fashion history, cultural studies, and consumer psychology enables the team to craft products that resonate with consumers on a deeper level. This mix of creativity, technical expertise, and market insight ensures that fashion designers not only keep up with trends but set them.

TECHNICAL DEPARTMENT

The Technical Department is essential for transforming design ideas into reality, making certain they can be executed effectively and efficiently. Its the primary duty of technologists is to ensure that designs are both practical and capable of being manufactured on a large scale. This involves creating detailed technical specifications, developing patterns, and overseeing the sample generation. The team guarantees that each item aligns with the brand's standards for quality, fit, and functionality while working closely with designers to convert creative concepts into straightforward, actionable guidelines for manufacturers.

Crucial skills for the technical team include expertise in pattern making, garment construction, and size grading. A thorough comprehension of textile characteristics and how fabrics behave is vital. Mastery of tools such as CAD (Computer Aided Designing) and pattern-making software is also necessary for generating accurate technical documentation. Moreover, meticulous attention to detail, problem-solving abilities, and strong communication skills are essential for addressing production issues and ensuring a smooth transition from design to manufacturing.

Additional understanding including expertise in sustainable manufacturing methods, advanced sewing techniques, and garment engineering can augment the team's capabilities. A solid understanding of international production standards and regulatory compliance is also critical to ensure that the final product satisfies global quality and safety requirements. By integrating these competencies, the technical department guarantees the production of high-quality garments that adapt to the fashion industry's continually changing demands.

PURCHASING DEPARTMENT

The Purchasing Department plays a crucial role in efficiently sourcing materials and services necessary for fashion production. Its primary responsibility is to acquire fabrics, trims, and other vital components, ensuring they adhere to required quality standards and are delivered punctually. This entails negotiating with suppliers, overseeing inventory management, and developing strong relationships with vendors. The department aims to secure advantageous terms concerning cost, quality, and delivery while efficiently managing OTB (Open To Buy) budgets and ensuring healthy profit margins, thus supporting the overall efficiency and profitability of the production process.

Essential skills for the purchasing team include effective negotiation strategies and a thorough understanding of textiles and garment manufacturing.

Expertise in inventory management and supply chain logistics is crucial for timely and cost-efficient procurement. Analytical abilities and meticulous attention to detail are necessary for monitoring supplier performance and managing financial plans. Strong communication skills are vital for collaborating with design, production, and other departments to meet all material requirements.

The team's efficiency can be significantly improved by gaining insights into sustainable and ethical sourcing practices, as the fashion industry transitions towards responsible manufacturing. Familiarity with global trade regulations, market dynamics, and procurement software enables the department to refine purchasing strategies. By integrating these varied skills, the purchasing team guarantees a continuous supply of high-quality materials essential for production in a rapidly changing industry.

QUALITY CONTROL DEPARTMENT

The Quality Control (QC) Department within the fashion sector plays a crucial role in ensuring that products adhere to predetermined standards prior to reaching consumers. Its main function is to assess and evaluate garments throughout the manufacturing process, beginning with raw materials and continuing through to finished products. The department establishes quality criteria, performs regular audits, and detects defects or irregularities. Through the application of strict quality assessments, the QC team helps prevent inferior products from being released into the market, protecting the brand's reputation and maintaining customer satisfaction.

Essential skills for the QC team include a thorough knowledge of textile characteristics, garment assembly, and quality requirements. Mastery of inspection tools to identify flaws is vital, as is meticulous attention to detail when scrutinizing products for any discrepancies from established specifications. Strong analytical abilities are important for assessing quality data and recommending enhancements. Effective communication is key for working alongside production teams to swiftly tackle and resolve quality concerns.

Understanding sustainable and ethical manufacturing practices enhances the team's effectiveness, particularly, as brands and consumers increasingly focus on environmental accountability. Being well-versed in global quality standards and regulations ensures compliance across different markets. Proficiency in data analysis and quality management frameworks, such as Six Sigma and ISO, contributes to process optimization and fosters ongoing improvement. By integrating these varied skills, the QC department guarantees consistent, high-quality output in the dynamic fashion industry.

QUALITY ASSURANCE DEPARTMENT

The Quality Assurance (QA) Department is crucial in the fashion sector, ensuring that every phase of the production process adheres to the highest quality standards. From the design phase through to the final product, QA is tasked with creating and implementing thorough quality management systems that ensure everything stays on course. This includes establishing clear quality criteria, conducting regular inspections, and putting proactive measures in place to avert defects. The objective is to reduce risks, improve product dependability, and maximize customer satisfaction.

An effective QA team has a comprehensive understanding of quality management concepts, garment construction techniques, and fabric characteristics. Proficiency in quality management systems like ISO, along with skills in auditing methods, is vital to maintain these standards. Accuracy is essential, as identifying potential problems early can help avoid expensive delays. Strong problem-solving abilities are equally important, allowing the team to develop and apply successful corrective measures. Clear communication is necessary to ensure all departments are on the same page regarding quality standards and processes.

In today's landscape, a diverse skill set is increasingly essential. As the fashion industry embraces sustainability and ethical practices, QA teams need to stay informed about these developments. Understanding global regulations and standards ensures that products comply with the expectations of international markets. Furthermore, skills in data analysis and continuous improvement techniques such as Six Sigma empower QA to refine processes and enhance quality consistently. By integrating these skills, QA teams remain flexible, delivering high-quality products that satisfy consumers and uphold the brand's reputation.

THE CORE PRODUCT DEVELOPMENT TEAM SYNERGY

Collaboration between the design, technical, purchasing, and quality teams is essential in the fashion industry for producing successful results. When these groups operate together, it promotes a smooth workflow where every stage, from ideation to final output, is maximized. The design team can closely collaborate with technical specialists to ensure the designs are practical, which facilitates efficient prototyping and allows for faster modifications. Input from the purchasing team ensures that the materials are both cost-effective and readily available, thus avoiding any potential delays. At the same time, the quality control team is involved from the start, ensuring that the final products meet the brand's standards. This collaboration not only shortens the time to market but also improves product quality and boosts customer satisfaction, ultimately enhancing a brand's reputation and success in the marketplace.

ESSENTIAL SUPPORT DEPARTMENTS

In addition to the core product development teams mentioned earlier—Design, Buying, Technical, and Quality — several supporting teams play crucial roles in ensuring successful product launches. These include Merchandise Planning, Visual Merchandising, Marketing, Human Resources, Finance, Information Technology, Shipping, and Warehousing. While these teams may not directly shape the product itself, they contribute significantly to the operational flow and success of product launches through their respective departments. Their roles encompass strategic planning, brand presentation, promotional activities, organizational support, financial management, technology integration, and logistics management, all of which are essential for a seamless product development and launch process.

MERCHANDISE PLANNING DEPARTMENT

The Merchandise Planning Department in the fashion sector plays an essential role in guaranteeing that products are supplied in the appropriate amounts, at the right moments, and according to consumer preferences. The primary responsibility of the department is to develop and implement merchandise strategies that align with the brand's financial goals. This involves examining sales data, forecasting trends, and overseeing inventory needs. Working alongside the buying, design, and marketing teams aids in creating assortments that not only meet customer desires but also enhance profitability while reducing excess stock.

To be effective, a merchandise planning team must possess strong analytical abilities and a comprehensive understanding of market trends and consumer habits. Proficiency in planning software and data analysis tools is crucial for reliable forecasting and inventory management. Attention to detail and numerical proficiency are vital for preparing meticulous plans and assessing sales performance. Moreover, effective communication and teamwork skills are important to ensure that merchandise strategies are consistent with the company's overall objectives. Enhancing this skill set with knowledge in retail mathematics, financial planning, and supply chain management further boosts the team's effectiveness. As online sales grow, expertise in e-commerce methods and an emphasis on sustainability have also become essential, enabling the department to successfully navigate the rapidly changing fashion industry.

VISUAL MERCHANDISE DEPARTMENT

The Visual Merchandising Department within the fashion sector plays a vital role in creating an engaging and visually appealing shopping atmosphere. Its primary task is to design and implement store displays and layouts that catch the attention of customers and enhance their shopping experience. This encompasses the creation of striking window displays, the arrangement of store layouts, and the strategic placement of products to emphasize key items and boost sales. The department works closely with marketing and sales teams to ensure that the visual concepts are in harmony with the brand's messaging and promotional efforts.

Essential skills for a visual merchandising team include creativity and a sharp sense of design. Being proficient in design software and tools is important for developing and showcasing visual concepts. A strong attention to detail and an insight into consumer behavior are crucial for ensuring that displays are not only attractive but also effective in swaying purchasing decisions. Effective project management and organizational skills are necessary for implementing visual merchandising strategies within established timelines and budgets.

Further skills that can enhance the success of a visual merchandising team include knowledge of graphic design, interior design, and lighting techniques, all of which can enhance the quality of displays. An understanding of digital and interactive merchandising strategies is increasingly significant as technology continues to impact the retail landscape. Familiarity with brand identity and marketing principles ensures that visual merchandising aligns with the brand's larger business objectives, ultimately leading to increased sales and customer loyalty.

MARKETING DEPARTMENT

The fashion industry's Marketing Department is vital for successfully promoting brands and, products to the appropriate audience. Its primary function is to develop and execute marketing strategies that enhance brand exposure, increase sales, and cultivate customer loyalty. This involves conducting thorough market research to grasp consumer behavior and trends, creating focused promotional campaigns, and overseeing both digital and traditional advertising channels. In addition, the department manages public relations, collaborates with influencers, and coordinates events to maintain a consistent brand image and strengthen consumer engagement.

Essential skills for an effective fashion marketing team include creativity alongside a strategic approach. Proficiency in digital marketing tools, social media channels, and content creation is crucial for engaging consumers through online platforms. Strong analytical skills are important for evaluating the effectiveness of campaigns and adjusting strategies based on performance metrics. Communication and storytelling abilities are necessary for expressing the brand's message and values across various touch points.

To further enhance the team's efficiency, knowledge in trend forecasting, consumer psychology and retail analytics allows for anticipating market trends, while expertise in brand management and crisis communication helps maintain a uniform and resilient brand voice. Furthermore, comprehension of packaging design and product presentation improves the overall customer experience, which is key to driving consumer loyalty and sales within a competitive fashion landscape.

HUMAN RESOURCE DEPARTMENT

The Human Resource (HR) Department in the fashion sector is essential for managing talent and ensuring that the workforce aligns with the company's objectives. Its responsibilities include recruiting, nurturing, and keeping employees who are a good fit for the organization's culture. This encompasses overseeing recruitment initiatives, onboarding freshly hired employees, and establishing training programs to boost skills and performance. HR also cultivates a supportive workplace to promote productivity and employee satisfaction.

Key competencies for an HR team in fashion encompass strong interpersonal skills, proficiency in recruitment and talent acquisition, as well as knowledge of employment regulations. Having effective communication and conflict resolution abilities is crucial for addressing employee issues and sustaining positive relationships. Additionally, expertise in compensation, benefits administration, and succession planning is vital for attracting and retaining top talent, while an understanding of diversity and inclusion practices fosters creativity and innovation. These competencies empower the HR department to build a motivated workforce that propels the success of the fashion enterprise.

FINANCE DEPARTMENT

The Finance Department is essential for preserving the financial health and stability of the organization.

Its primary duty involves managing financial planning, budgeting, and forecasting to ensure the company achieves its financial goals. This encompasses the preparation of financial reports, assessment of financial performance, and providing strategic insights to support decision-making processes. The department is also responsible for overseeing cash flow, controlling costs, and tracking profitability to improve financial results and enhance shareholder value.

Essential skills for a finance team in the fashion industry include a solid understanding of accounting principles, financial analysis, and reporting. Competence in financial modeling and the use of tools such as ERP (Enterprise Resource Management) systems is vital for precise financial planning. Analytical skills and meticulous attention to detail are required for interpreting financial data and identifying areas for improvement. Strong communication abilities are important for conveying financial information to stakeholders and influencing business decisions. Furthermore, knowledge in cost management, risk mitigation, and compliance ensures that the company adheres to regulatory standards and minimizes financial risks. A thorough understanding of international finance is crucial for fashion companies that operate globally. By integrating these varied skills, the finance department can offer clear financial guidance and contribute to the sustainable growth and profitability of the fashion industry.

INFORMATION TECHNOLOGY DEPARTMENT

The Information Technology (IT) Department within the fashion sector plays a crucial role in leveraging technology to enhance business operations and functions. Its main duty is to oversee the design, implementation, and maintenance of IT systems and infrastructure that support operations in the fashion industry. This entails managing networks, servers, and databases, as well as offering technical support to ensure smooth daily operations. The department also plays a key role in sustaining e-commerce platforms, inventory management systems, and digital marketing tools to boost customer engagement and optimize business processes.

Essential skills for an IT team in the fashion industry include expertise in IT infrastructure management, system administration, and cyber security. Knowledge of programming languages like Java or Python, combined with experience in cloud computing platforms such as AWS or Azure, is vital for developing and maintaining scalable solutions. The ability to solve problems and troubleshoot quickly is critical for reducing disruptions and ensuring ongoing operations.

Effective communication skills are also essential for working with different departments to understand their technological needs and provide solutions that align with business objectives.

To further enhance the team's effectiveness, an understanding of data analytics and business intelligence facilitates data-driven decision-making and improved operational efficiency. Proficiency in UX design and mobile app development is increasingly important as brands broaden their digital footprint. Awareness of emerging technologies such as artificial intelligence (AI) and the Internet of Things (IoT) allows for innovative solutions that enhance customer experiences and business agility. Collectively, these skills establish the IT department as a pivotal force in the fashion industry, driving digital transformation and adapting to changing consumer demands.

SHIPPING DEPARTMENT

The Shipping Department manages and oversees the logistics of transporting products from manufacturers to retailers or directly to consumers. Its primary duty is to guarantee prompt and effective deliveries while controlling costs and upholding quality standards. This includes coordinating with suppliers, carriers, and distribution centers to organize shipments, oversee inventory, and monitor orders throughout the supply chain. The department also handles customs clearance for international shipments and manages returns or exchanges, ensuring a seamless experience for customers.

Essential skills for a shipping team in fashion comprise knowledge in logistics management, supply chain coordination, and transportation logistics. Familiarity with shipping regulations and customs processes is crucial for dealing with international trade and adhering to import/export laws. Strong organizational abilities and meticulous attention to detail are imperative for managing numerous shipments and maintaining accurate inventory records. Excellent communication and problem-solving skills are essential for resolving issues such as delays or damaged goods, minimizing disruptions, and ensuring customer satisfaction.

Additional abilities can further boost the team's effectiveness. Expertise in warehouse management systems (WMS) and inventory control software aids in optimizing operations. Awareness of sustainable logistics practices and reverse logistics is becoming increasingly important as companies focus on environmental responsibility and effective returns management. Furthermore, negotiation skills and contract management with shipping carriers can help lower costs and enhance logistics performance. Collectively, these skills empower the shipping department to address the fashion industry's intricate demands, guaranteeing timely delivery while optimizing supply chain functions.

WAREHOUSING DEPARTMENT

Warehousing in the fashion sector is tasked with the storage, organization, and distribution of products within a warehouse facility. Its main role is to effectively manage inventory to guarantee that products are readily available for distribution or retail delivery. This includes receiving incoming shipments, checking goods for quality and quantity, and placing them in specific locations within the warehouse. The department also manages order picking, packing, and shipping processes to fulfill customer orders accurately and efficiently.

Key skills required for a warehousing team in the fashion sector encompass inventory management, warehouse operations, and logistics coordination. Being proficient with warehouse management systems (WMS) and inventory tracking software is essential for keeping accurate inventory records and optimizing storage space. Attention to detail and strong organizational abilities are critical for effectively managing stock levels and ensuring that goods are readily accessible for order fulfillment. Strong communication and teamwork skills are crucial for collaborating with other departments, such as shipping and purchasing, to satisfy customer needs and achieve operational objectives.

A variety of skills further improve the effectiveness of a warehousing team. Knowledge of supply chain logistics and distribution strategies aids in streamlining warehouse operations and enhancing order fulfillment efficiency. Familiarity with health and safety regulations ensures a secure working environment for warehouse personnel and compliance with workplace guidelines. Furthermore, expertise in process improvement and continuous optimization empowers the team to identify and apply efficiencies that lower costs and boost productivity. Merging these diverse skills enables the warehousing department to assist the fashion business by maintaining smooth inventory flow, optimizing storage and distribution processes, and ultimately ensuring timely and precise delivery of products to customers.

CHAPTER 11

ULTIMATE TOOLS –
QUALITY MANAGEMENT

THE 7 QUALITY TOOLS

The seven tools of quality, often referred to as the "Ishikawa's Seven Basic Tools Of Quality," are essential instruments used in quality management and continuous improvement processes. These tools help organizations identify, analyze, and solve quality-related issues.

Each of the Seven Quality Tools has evolved over time which are originally developed by multiple contributors. However, Dr. Kaoru Ishikawa is largely responsible for consolidating these tools into the "Seven Quality Tools" and promoting them as essential techniques for quality improvement across industries.

Kaoru Ishikawa, a pioneering Japanese engineering professor, compiled the "seven quality tools" (7 QC tools) in the 1950s to promote successful quality control across industries. These tools, built for simplicity and broad applicability, were meant to empower workers from various technical backgrounds to discover, assess, and fix quality concerns in a methodical manner. The 7 QC tools established a culture of continuous improvement in manufacturing and other sectors around the world by allowing for a disciplined approach to quality management.

The seven tools are:

1. Cause-and-effect Diagram (also know as - Ishikawa or Fishbone Diagram): This tool helps identify potential causes of a problem by categorizing causes into groups, making it easier to pinpoint root causes.

2. Check Sheet: A structured, prepared form for collecting and analyzing data. It is used to record and compile data in real-time at the location where the data is generated.

3. Control Chart: A graph used to study how a process changes over time. Data are plotted in time order, and control limits are used to detect significant variations that may indicate problems.

4. Histogram: A type of bar chart that shows the frequency distribution of a dataset. It helps visualize the shape and spread of continuous data, making it easier to identify patterns and outliers.

5. Pareto Chart: A bar graph that identifies and prioritizes problems or causes in a process. It is based on the Pareto principle (80/20 rule), which states that 80% of problems are often due to 20% of causes.

6. Scatter Diagram: A graphical representation of the relationship between two variables. It helps identify correlations and potential cause-and-effect relationships between variables.

7. Flowchart (Process Diagram): A visual representation of the steps in a process. It helps understand and analyze the workflow, identify bottlenecks, and improve efficiency.

These tools are fundamental for quality control and improvement efforts across various industries, providing a systematic approach to problem-solving and decision-making. Let's explore each of them in detail.

CAUSE AND EFFECT DIAGRAM

The Cause-and-Effect Diagram, also known as the Ishikawa or Fishbone Diagram, was developed by Dr. Kaoru Ishikawa, a prominent Japanese quality management innovator, in the 1950s. Ishikawa introduced this tool as part of his efforts to enhance quality control processes. He was deeply influenced by the principles of W. Edwards Deming and Joseph Juran, who were instrumental in shaping modern quality management practices. Ishikawa's diagram was designed to systematically identify and organize potential causes of problems or defects in a process, making it easier to pinpoint root causes and implement effective solutions.

In the fashion industry, the Cause-and-Effect Diagram plays a crucial role in quality control and continuous improvement. Fashion businesses face numerous challenges, such as maintaining high-quality standards, managing production costs, and meeting tight deadlines. By using this diagram, fashion professionals can visually map out all possible factors that might be contributing to issues like production delays, quality defects, or supply chain inefficiencies. The diagram typically categorizes causes into major groups such as Materials, Methods, Machines, Measurement, Environment, and People (Manpower), allowing for a comprehensive analysis.

For instance, if a fashion company is experiencing a high rate of defective garments, the Ishikawa Diagram can help identify whether the root cause lies in substandard raw materials, faulty machinery, inadequate worker training, or other factors. Each category in the diagram branches out into more specific potential causes, facilitating a thorough examination of the production process. By systematically investigating these potential causes, the company can implement targeted improvements, such as upgrading machinery, enhancing quality control measures, or providing additional training to employees.

Implementing the Cause-and-Effect Diagram in the fashion industry can lead to significant improvements in product quality and operational efficiency. By identifying and addressing the root causes of problems, fashion companies can reduce waste, minimize costs, and improve customer satisfaction. This methodical approach ensures that corrective actions are based on data and systematic analysis, rather than assumptions or guesswork. As a result, the fashion business can maintain high standards of quality while staying competitive in a fast-paced market.

CHECK LIST

The concept of the checklist has origins that trace back to the early 20th century, primarily within the field of aviation. Boeing developed a simple, step-by-step checklist for pilots to follow, ensuring that all critical procedures were completed. This drastically improved safety and efficiency in aviation and soon found applications in various industries globally. Dr. Walter A. Shewhart is credited with the concept of checklists.

In the fashion industry, the checklist is an invaluable tool for managing the numerous intricate processes involved in design, production, and quality control. Given the fast-paced nature of fashion, where trends change rapidly, and deadlines are tight, checklists help ensure that nothing is overlooked. They provide a structured way to manage tasks, track progress, and verify that all necessary steps are taken at each stage of the production process.

For example, during the garment production process, a checklist can be used to ensure quality and consistency. It can include items such as fabric inspection, pattern accuracy, stitching quality, and final product checks. Each step can be systematically ticked off, ensuring that standards are met before the garment moves on to the next phase. This reduces the risk of defects and ensures that issues if any, are identified and addressed promptly.

Checklists also play a critical role in the fashion industry's supply chain management. From verifying that materials are sourced from approved suppliers to ensuring that shipments meet delivery schedules, checklists help maintain order and accountability. By using checklists, fashion companies can streamline operations, reduce errors, and improve overall efficiency. This simple but methodical approach supports better planning and execution, ultimately leading to higher-quality products and increased customer satisfaction.

CONTROL CHART

The Control Chart, also known as the Shewhart Chart, was invented by Dr. Walter A. Shewhart in the early 1920s while he was working at Bell Telephone Laboratories. Shewhart was a physicist, engineer, and statistician who sought to improve manufacturing quality. He developed the Control Chart to monitor process variability and distinguish between common causes of variation (inherent to the process) and special causes (due to specific, identifiable factors). His work laid the foundation for modern statistical process control (SPC) and quality management practices, significantly influencing subsequent quality gurus like W. Edwards Deming.

In the fashion industry, the Control Chart is a powerful tool for maintaining and improving quality throughout the production process. Fashion manufacturing involves numerous variables, such as fabric quality, dye consistency, and stitching accuracy. Variations in these factors can lead to defects and inconsistencies in the final product. By utilizing Control Charts, fashion companies can monitor these variables in real-time and ensure that the process remains within acceptable limits.

For instance, a fashion manufacturer might use Control Charts to monitor the tensile strength of fabric during production. Data points are plotted on the chart over time, and min-max control limits are established based on historical data. If the tensile strength of the fabric stays within these control limits, the process is considered to be in control. However, if data points fall outside the control limits, it indicates that there may be a special cause of variation that needs to be investigated and corrected, such as a problem with the fabric supplier or a malfunction in the machinery.

Implementing Control Charts in the fashion industry helps in early detection of issues, allowing for timely interventions before defects become widespread. This proactive approach leads to more consistent product quality, reduced waste, and lower production costs. Additionally, maintaining tight control over production processes enhances the company's reputation for quality and reliability, which is crucial in a highly competitive market. Overall, Control Charts enable fashion businesses to achieve higher standards of quality and efficiency, contributing to their long-term success.

HISTOGRAM

The Histogram, a fundamental tool in statistical analysis, was developed by Karl Pearson in the late 19th century. Pearson, a pioneering British mathematician and biostatistician, introduced the histogram as a graphical representation of data distribution. His work in the field of statistics laid the groundwork for many modern statistical methods, and the histogram became a cornerstone for visualizing data distributions, helping to identify patterns, trends, and outliers.

In the fashion industry, histograms are essential for analyzing various aspects of production and quality control. They provide a visual summary of data, enabling fashion professionals to quickly understand the distribution and frequency of specific variables. This can be particularly useful for identifying variations in production processes and ensuring that quality standards are consistently met.

For example, a fashion company might use histograms to analyze the distribution of garment sizes produced in a batch. By plotting the frequency of each point of measure on a histogram, the company can easily see if the production is skewed towards a particular part or if it follows the expected distribution. If the histogram reveals that certain discrepancies are being produced more frequently than others, it may indicate an issue with the cutting patterns or machinery settings, which can then be addressed to ensure a balanced production.

Histograms are also valuable for quality control in the fashion industry. They can be used to monitor the consistency of fabric thickness, color uniformity, or stitching quality. By regularly collecting and plotting this data, companies can detect any deviations from the standard specifications. If a histogram shows an unusual spread or shift in the data, it signals that there may be a problem in the production process that needs investigation. This allows for timely corrective actions, minimizing defects and ensuring that the final products meet the desired quality standards.

Overall, histograms help fashion companies maintain control over their production processes by providing a clear and immediate visual representation of data. This facilitates informed decision-making, leading to improved quality, efficiency, and customer satisfaction. By leveraging the insights gained from histograms, fashion businesses can continually refine their operations and uphold high standards in a competitive market.

PARETO CHART

The Pareto Chart, named after the Italian economist Vilfredo Pareto, has its origins in Pareto's observation in the early 20th century that approximately 80% of Italy's land was owned by 20% of the population. This principle, now known as the Pareto Principle or the 80/20 rule, was later generalized by quality management pioneer Joseph M. Juran. Juran applied the principle to quality control, suggesting that roughly 80% of problems are caused by 20% of causes. He developed the Pareto Chart as a visual tool to identify and prioritize these critical causes, facilitating more efficient problem-solving and resource allocation.

In the fashion industry, the Pareto Chart is a powerful tool for quality management and process improvement. It helps fashion companies identify the most significant issues affecting production and quality. By categorizing and ranking problems based on their frequency or impact, the Pareto Chart enables companies to focus their efforts on the few key areas that will yield the most substantial improvements.

For instance, a fashion company might use a Pareto Chart to analyze customer complaints about their products. By categorizing complaints into types such as stitching defects, size inconsistencies, fabric quality, and color discrepancies, the company can plot these issues on a Pareto Chart. The chart will visually highlight which types of complaints are most frequent or have the most significant impact on customer satisfaction. If stitching defects and size inconsistencies make up 80% of the complaints, the company knows to prioritize improvements in these areas.

Using the Pareto Chart allows fashion companies to allocate resources more effectively, targeting the root causes of the most significant problems. This focused approach can lead to substantial improvements in product quality and operational efficiency. For example, addressing the top causes of defects might involve investing in better machinery, enhancing worker training, or improving quality control procedures. By systematically tackling the most critical issues, the company can reduce defects, improve product quality, and increase customer satisfaction.

Overall, the Pareto Chart provides a clear and actionable way for fashion companies to identify and address the most impactful issues in their processes. By concentrating on the vital few causes of problems, they can achieve significant improvements with relatively less effort, enhancing their competitiveness and reputation in the market.

SCATTER DIAGRAM

The Scatter Diagram, also known as a scatter plot, traces its origins back to the early 20th century and was popularized by the pioneering work of British statistician Sir Francis Galton. Galton used scatter diagrams to study the relationship between different variables, particularly in his work on heredity. This graphical representation allows for the visualization of correlations between two variables, helping to identify patterns, trends, and possible cause-and-effect relationships.

In the fashion industry, scatter diagrams are used for analyzing the relationships between various factors affecting production, quality, and sales. By plotting data points on a graph, fashion companies can visually inspect how changes in one variable may impact another. This analysis is crucial for identifying areas where improvements can be made, optimizing processes, and enhancing product quality.

For example, a fashion company might use a scatter diagram to examine the relationship between fabric quality and defect rates in finished garments. By plotting the defect rates against fabric quality ratings for different batches, the company can see if there is a correlation between lower-quality fabric and higher defect rates. If a strong positive correlation is identified, it suggests that improving fabric quality could lead to a reduction in defects.

Scatter diagrams are also useful for analyzing production efficiency. A fashion company could plot the time taken to produce a garment against the number of defects found in each batch. If a scatter diagram reveals that shorter production times are associated with higher defect rates, it indicates that rushing the production process may be compromising quality. The company can then investigate further to find a balance between speed and quality, ensuring efficient production without sacrificing standards.

Overall, scatter diagrams provide a clear visual representation of data relationships, enabling informed decision-making and targeted improvements. By understanding and leveraging these correlations, fashion businesses can optimize their processes, enhance product quality, and ultimately increase customer satisfaction. This data-driven approach helps maintain competitive advantage in the fast-paced fashion industry.

FLOWCHART

The flowchart, a visual representation of a process, was first introduced by Frank Gilbreth and his wife Lillian Gilbreth, pioneers in the field of industrial engineering and management. In the early 1920s, they developed the "Process Flow Chart" to document and analyze work processes in various industries. This tool aimed to break down and visualize each step in a process, highlighting inefficiencies and areas for improvement. Their work significantly influenced the field of process engineering and management, leading to widespread adoption of flowcharts in various industries for process analysis and optimization.

In the fashion industry, flowcharts are essential for mapping out the complex processes involved in design, production, and distribution. By providing a clear visual representation of each step in these processes, flowcharts help fashion companies identify bottlenecks, redundancies, and inefficiencies. This systematic approach facilitates better understanding and management of workflows, leading to more efficient and streamlined operations.

For instance, a fashion company can use a flowchart to map out the entire garment production process, from design conceptualization to final quality inspection. Each step, such as fabric selection, cutting, stitching, and finishing, is represented visually, showing the sequence of operations and decision points. By analyzing this flowchart, the company can identify stages where delays or errors frequently occur, such as bottlenecks in the cutting phase or quality issues during stitching.

Flowcharts are also valuable for improving communication and coordination within the fashion industry. They provide a common visual language that can be easily understood by all stakeholders, from designers and production managers to quality control teams and suppliers. This clarity helps ensure that everyone is on the same page, reducing misunderstandings and facilitating smoother collaboration. For example, when introducing a new product line, a flowchart can help coordinate the efforts of different departments, ensuring that all necessary steps are completed in the correct order and on schedule.

Overall, the use of flowcharts in the fashion industry leads to improved efficiency, reduced errors, and enhanced quality control. By providing a clear and detailed visualization of processes, flowcharts enable fashion companies to optimize their operations, leading to faster production times, lower costs, and higher-quality products. This, in turn, helps fashion businesses remain competitive in a rapidly evolving market.

CHAPTER 12

PRECISION PERFORMANCE – OPERATIONAL EFFICIENCY

THE IMPACT OF TOOLS

Using the right tools in any situation transforms complexity into clarity, making even the most challenging tasks manageable. These tools break down the workload into simple, achievable chunks, allowing for focused effort on each part rather than being overwhelmed by the whole. This structured approach not only enhances efficiency but also builds confidence as small milestones are reached, leading to steady progress and a strong sense of accomplishment.

The tools featured in Chapter 11 are essential for achieving maximum efficiency, but their true power unfolds when combined with the following exercises listed below. Applied in the right manner and at the right moments, these exercises foster significant improvements and transformative results. Regular follow-ups with the team reinforce these changes, ensuring that progress is not only achieved but sustained over time, creating a culture of continuous improvement and collaboration.

CRITICAL PATH ANALYSIS (CPA)

Maintaining a "Critical Path" is crucial in the fashion industry for efficient project management and timely product launches. The critical path represents the sequence of tasks that directly influence the project's duration. By identifying and focusing on these tasks, fashion businesses can ensure that essential activities are prioritized, preventing delays. This is particularly important in fashion, where trends shift quickly, and the timely release of new collections is vital for maintaining market relevance.

Effective use of the critical path in fashion operations facilitates better coordination among various departments, such as design, production, and marketing. If the design phase is delayed, it will cascade through the entire schedule, affecting production and launch dates. By concentrating on the critical path, managers can allocate resources more efficiently and develop contingency plans for potential delays. This proactive strategy helps maintain smooth operations and ensures deadlines are met, capitalizing on current fashion trends.

Moreover, the critical path method enhances communication and collaboration across the fashion supply chain. Projects often involve multiple stakeholders, including designers, fabric suppliers, manufacturers, and retailers. Sharing the critical path with all parties ensures a clear understanding of roles and deadlines, reducing the risk of miscommunication and ensuring each step is completed on time. This synchronization is crucial for delivering collections promptly and avoiding the high costs associated with missed deadlines.

Finally, the critical path approach provides a framework for continuous improvement in fashion operations. Analyzing the critical path post-project completion helps identify where delays occurred, allowing companies to implement strategies to mitigate these in future projects. This iterative refinement process streamlines operations, reduces time-to-market, and enhances overall efficiency. In an industry where speed and agility are key competitive advantages, maintaining an accurate and dynamic critical path is indispensable for long-term success.

POST SEASON ANALYSIS

Post Season Analysis in the fashion industry encompasses several critical aspects that collectively contribute to strategic decision-making and continuous improvement across product development teams. Firstly, it evaluates product performance by scrutinizing sales data, customer feedback, and market reception. This assessment not only identifies which products resonated well with consumers but also highlights areas for improvement in terms of design, functionality, or marketing approach. By understanding the factors driving successful products versus those that underperformed, fashion brands can refine their future product offerings to better meet customer expectations and market demands.

Furthermore, the analysis delves into identifying emerging trends that gained popularity and those that failed to capture consumer interest. This trend analysis guides future design decisions, ensuring that upcoming collections are aligned with evolving consumer preferences and fashion trends. Simultaneously, evaluating inventory management effectiveness through reviews of stock levels and sell-through rates informs adjustments in production volumes, assortment planning, and distribution strategies. This optimization minimizes excess inventory costs and enhances overall supply chain efficiency, enabling brands to respond more agilely to market fluctuations and consumer demand shifts.

Customer insights gleaned from data on preferences, buying patterns, and demographic trends provide invaluable guidance for targeted marketing and product development strategies. By understanding consumer behavior and preferences, brands can tailor their offerings and marketing messages more effectively, enhancing customer satisfaction and loyalty. This customer-centric approach is complemented by rigorous quality control assessments that identify manufacturing or design flaws. Addressing these issues proactively improves product quality, reduces returns, and mitigates customer dissatisfaction, thereby bolstering brand reputation and long-term profitability.

Financial analysis plays a pivotal role in optimizing pricing strategies, budget allocations, and profitability goals for future seasons. By scrutinizing costs, margins, and overall financial performance, fashion brands can make informed decisions that support sustainable growth and financial health. Additionally, gathering feedback from suppliers and partners sheds light on operational efficiencies, supply chain challenges, and opportunities for collaboration enhancement. This collaborative feedback loop fosters stronger partnerships, improves supply chain resilience, and supports continuous improvement initiatives across the organization.

Incorporating assessments of marketing effectiveness, sustainability practices, and team learning further enriches the Post Season Analysis process. Evaluating the impact of marketing campaigns helps refine future strategies, enhancing brand visibility and market penetration. Assessing sustainability practices ensures alignment with environmental and ethical standards, meeting regulatory requirements and consumer expectations. Finally, recording insights and fostering a culture of continuous learning and development among product development teams promotes innovation, agility, and excellence in delivering fashion collections that resonate with consumers globally.

STANDARD OPERATING PROCEDURE (SOP)

Establishing Standard Operating Procedures (SOPs) is crucial for maintaining consistency and efficiency in any organization. SOPs provide detailed, written instructions to achieve uniformity in the performance of specific functions. By standardizing processes, organizations ensure that tasks are performed consistently and correctly, regardless of who completes them. This consistency is essential for maintaining quality, reducing errors, and ensuring that all employees adhere to best practices, which ultimately enhances overall productivity and reliability.

SOPs also play a significant role in training and onboarding new employees. Clear, step-by-step instructions make it easier for new hires to understand their roles and responsibilities quickly. This reduces the learning curve and helps new employees become productive more rapidly. Additionally, SOPs serve as a valuable reference for existing employees, providing a reliable source of information when questions or uncertainties arise. This helps maintain operational continuity and reduces the dependency on individual knowledge.

Moreover, SOPs contribute to compliance with industry regulations and standards. Many industries, such as healthcare, manufacturing, and finance, have strict regulatory requirements that organizations must adhere to. SOPs ensure that all processes are performed in compliance with these regulations, thereby reducing the risk of legal issues and penalties. By documenting procedures, organizations can also provide evidence of compliance during audits and inspections, demonstrating their commitment to regulatory standards and operational excellence.

Finally, SOPs facilitate continuous improvement within organizations. By regularly reviewing and updating SOPs, companies can identify inefficiencies and implement improvements to enhance their processes. This iterative process ensures that operations remain efficient and effective over time. Furthermore, involving employees in the development and review of SOPs fosters a culture of continuous improvement and accountability. By empowering employees to contribute to process enhancements, organizations can drive innovation and maintain a competitive edge in their industry.

KEY PERFORMANCE INDICATORS (KPI)

Establishing Key Performance Indicators (KPIs) is vital for measuring and managing the performance of any organization. KPIs are quantifiable metrics that reflect the critical success factors of an organization. By setting and monitoring KPIs, organizations can objectively evaluate their progress toward strategic goals and make data-driven decisions. This helps ensure that all efforts are aligned with the company's vision and objectives, fostering a focused and cohesive approach to achieving desired outcomes.

KPIs are also instrumental in identifying areas for improvement. By tracking performance against predefined benchmarks, organizations can pinpoint weaknesses and inefficiencies. This enables managers to address issues proactively and implement corrective actions before they escalate into significant problems. Regularly reviewing KPIs provides valuable insights into operational performance and helps organizations adapt to changing circumstances and market conditions, ensuring sustained growth and competitiveness.

Furthermore, KPIs enhance accountability within an organization. When employees understand the specific metrics by which their performance is measured, they are more likely to take ownership of their responsibilities and strive for excellence. Clear, well-defined KPIs create a transparent environment where everyone knows what is expected of them. This transparency not only motivates employees but also fosters a culture of accountability, where individuals are encouraged to contribute to the organization's success.

Finally, KPIs facilitate effective communication and alignment across different departments and teams. By establishing common performance metrics, organizations ensure that all teams are working toward the same goals. This alignment is crucial for maintaining cohesion and ensuring that efforts across the organization are complementary rather than conflicting. Regular KPI reviews and updates keep everyone informed about progress and highlight areas where collaboration is needed. This fosters a unified approach to achieving organizational objectives and helps maintain a high level of performance across the board.

FIVE "S" (5S)

The "5S" methodology is a systematic approach to workplace organization and efficiency, originating from Japan. It comprises five steps: Sort, Set in Order, Shine, Standardize, and Sustain. "Sort" involves removing unnecessary items from the workspace. "Set in Order" focuses on organizing remaining items for easy access. "Shine" entails cleaning and inspecting the workspace regularly. "Standardize" involves creating consistent procedures for performing the first three steps. Finally,

"Sustain" requires maintaining and reviewing these standards to ensure long-term adherence.

Implementing 5S can significantly enhance organizational efficiency. By eliminating clutter and organizing the workspace, employees can find tools and materials quickly, reducing time wasted searching for items. This streamlined environment enables smoother workflows and minimizes interruptions, leading to increased productivity. A well-organized workspace also reduces the likelihood of errors and accidents, contributing to higher quality and safety standards.

Moreover, 5S fosters a culture of continuous improvement. Regular cleaning and inspection (Shine) help identify potential issues before they escalate, allowing for proactive maintenance and problem-solving. Standardizing processes ensures that best practices are consistently followed, leading to more reliable and predictable outcomes. This emphasis on standardization and improvement encourages employees to take ownership of their work environment and actively seek ways to enhance efficiency and effectiveness. The benefits of 5S extend beyond immediate operational improvements. A clean, organized workspace boosts employee morale and satisfaction, creating a more pleasant and motivating work environment. This positive atmosphere can lead to higher employee retention and engagement.

Additionally, the principles of 5S can be applied to various aspects of an organization, from office settings to manufacturing floors, making it a versatile tool for driving excellence. By embedding the 5S methodology into their culture, organizations can achieve sustained improvements in efficiency, quality, and employee well-being.

FAILURE MODE AND EFFECTS ANALYSIS (FMEA)

Failure Mode and Effect Analysis (FMEA) is a systematic tool used to identify potential failures in a process, product, or system and assess their impact. By examining possible failure modes and their effects, organizations can proactively address issues before they occur. FMEA helps prioritize risks based on their severity, occurrence, and detectability, enabling teams to focus on the most critical areas. This approach enhances reliability and safety, which is crucial for maintaining high standards and customer satisfaction.

Implementing FMEA in any organization begins with assembling a cross-functional team to analyze the process or product. Each potential failure mode is identified and evaluated for its potential effects on the overall system. The team then assigns a Risk Priority Number (RPN) to each failure mode by multiplying the ratings of severity, occurrence, and detectability.

This numerical value helps prioritize which issues need immediate attention. By addressing high RPNs, organizations can significantly reduce the risk of failures.

FMEA also promotes a proactive culture of continuous improvement. By regularly conducting FMEA, organizations can identify trends and recurring issues, leading to systemic improvements rather than temporary fixes. This iterative process ensures that the organization continuously refines its processes and products, enhancing overall quality and performance. Moreover, FMEA documentation provides a valuable reference for future projects, enabling teams to learn from past experiences and avoid repeating mistakes.

The benefits of FMEA extend across various industries, from manufacturing and healthcare to software development and aerospace. For example, in manufacturing, FMEA can prevent costly defects and production downtime by identifying potential equipment failures. In healthcare, it can enhance patient safety by anticipating and mitigating risks in medical procedures. By integrating FMEA into their quality management systems, organizations can achieve higher reliability, safety, and customer satisfaction. Ultimately, FMEA is a powerful tool for managing risk and driving continuous improvement, for any organization aiming for excellence.

ROOT CAUSE ANALYSIS (RCA)

Root Cause Analysis (RCA) is a methodical approach used to identify the underlying causes of problems or defects in an organization. By focusing on the root cause rather than just addressing the symptoms, RCA aims to prevent the recurrence of issues. This process involves collecting data, analyzing the problem, identifying the root cause, and implementing corrective actions. RCA is critical for improving processes, enhancing quality, and ensuring long-term solutions rather than temporary fixes.

The first step in RCA is to clearly define the problem. This involves gathering detailed information about the issue, including when it occurred, the circumstances surrounding it, and its impact. Once the problem is well-defined, the analysis phase begins, often using tools like the "5 Whys" or fishbone diagrams (Ishikawa diagrams). These tools help systematically explore the possible causes by repeatedly asking why the problem occurred, drilling down to the fundamental root cause.

Once the root cause is identified, the next step is to develop and implement corrective actions. These actions should address the root cause directly to prevent the issue from recurring. It's essential to involve relevant stakeholders in this process to ensure that the solutions are practical and effective. After implementation, the effectiveness of these actions should be monitored and reviewed to confirm that the problem has been resolved. This step is crucial for validating that the root cause has been addressed and that the corrective measures are sustainable.

RCA can be used effectively in any organization by integrating it into the regular problem-solving processes. For example, in manufacturing, RCA can reduce defects and downtime by addressing the root causes of equipment failures. In healthcare, it can improve patient safety by identifying the underlying causes of medical errors. Regularly conducting RCA helps build a culture of continuous improvement and accountability. By focusing on root causes, organizations can achieve more significant and lasting improvements, enhancing overall performance and efficiency.

CORRECTIVE ACTION AND PREVENTIVE ACTION (CAPA)

Corrective Action and Preventive Action (CAPA) is a systematic approach used in quality management to address and eliminate causes of non-conformities or other undesirable situations. Corrective actions aim to rectify existing issues, while preventive actions focus on avoiding potential problems before they occur. CAPA is essential for continuous improvement and compliance with industry standards, ensuring that organizations maintain high quality and operational efficiency.

The first step in the CAPA process is to identify and document the issue or potential risk. This involves detailed analysis to understand the problem's root cause, using tools like Root Cause Analysis (RCA). For corrective actions, the focus is on identifying why a problem occurred and implementing steps to fix it. For preventive actions, the focus shifts to identifying potential risks and developing strategies to prevent them. Clear documentation of this analysis is crucial for tracking and evaluating the effectiveness of CAPA efforts.

Once the root cause or potential risk is identified, the next step is to develop and implement appropriate actions. Corrective actions might include process changes, retraining employees, or equipment modifications to eliminate the root cause of a problem. Preventive actions might involve risk assessments, process improvements, or new quality control measures to avoid potential issues. It is important to involve relevant stakeholders in this process to ensure that the solutions are practical, comprehensive, and effective.

Monitoring and reviewing the effectiveness of CAPA measures is essential for ensuring long-term success. After implementing corrective and preventive actions, organizations must track their outcomes to verify that the issues have been resolved and that similar problems will not recur. Regular reviews and updates of CAPA procedures help maintain their relevance and effectiveness over time. By embedding CAPA into their quality management systems, organizations can achieve sustained improvements in quality and performance, enhance customer satisfaction, and ensure compliance with regulatory requirements. This proactive approach to problem-solving and risk management is fundamental to maintaining high standards and continuous improvement in any organization.

SUPPLIER SCORE CARDS (SSC)

Supplier scorecards are tools used by organizations to evaluate and manage the performance of their suppliers based on predefined metrics and criteria. These scorecards provide a structured framework for assessing various aspects of supplier performance, such as quality, delivery reliability, cost, responsiveness, and compliance with contractual terms. By systematically tracking and analyzing supplier performance, organizations can make informed decisions regarding supplier relationships, improve collaboration, and drive continuous improvement in their supply chain.

The key components of a supplier scorecard typically include quantitative measures, such as on-time delivery rates, defect rates, lead times, and cost-effectiveness. Qualitative factors, such as communication effectiveness, responsiveness to issues, and innovation capabilities, may also be included to provide a comprehensive assessment of supplier performance. Each metric is assigned a weight or importance level based on its impact on overall supply chain effectiveness and organizational goals.

Effectively using supplier scorecards involves regular monitoring and evaluation of supplier performance against established metrics. This process allows organizations to identify top-performing suppliers, recognize areas for improvement, and address any issues or discrepancies promptly. By establishing clear performance expectations and benchmarks through scorecards, organizations can foster accountability and transparency in supplier relationships, leading to mutual trust and collaboration.

Moreover, supplier scorecards enable data-driven decision-making in supplier selection and management processes. They provide objective insights into supplier capabilities and performance trends over time, facilitating strategic sourcing decisions and contract negotiations. By leveraging scorecard data, organizations can identify opportunities for cost savings, risk mitigation, and operational efficiencies within their supply chain network.

Ultimately, supplier scorecards support continuous improvement initiatives by encouraging ongoing dialogue and collaboration between buyers and suppliers. Regular feedback based on scorecard evaluations helps suppliers understand expectations and areas needing improvement, fostering a culture of continuous learning and enhancement. This collaborative approach not only strengthens supplier relationships but also enhances overall supply chain resilience and competitiveness in the market.

KAIZEN

Kaizen is a Japanese term meaning "continuous improvement" and is a philosophy that focuses on small, incremental changes to improve efficiency and quality within an organization. Unlike large-scale transformations, Kaizen emphasizes the value of making consistent, small improvements that accumulate over time. This approach involves everyone in the organization, from top management to front-line workers, fostering a culture of collective responsibility and proactive problem-solving. By continuously seeking ways to enhance processes, products, and services, Kaizen helps organizations remain competitive and adaptive.

Implementing Kaizen brings numerous benefits, starting with improved operational efficiency. By encouraging employees to identify and eliminate waste, streamline processes, and optimize workflows, Kaizen leads to significant time and cost savings. These incremental improvements can result in more effective use of resources, reduced downtime, and increased productivity. Additionally, because changes are small and continuous, they are often easier to implement and less disruptive than large-scale overhauls.

Another significant benefit of Kaizen is enhanced employee engagement and morale. Involving employees in the improvement process gives them a sense of ownership and pride in their work. When employees see their suggestions being implemented and making a positive impact, it boosts their motivation and satisfaction. This participative approach not only improves individual and team performance but also fosters a collaborative and innovative work culture. Employees feel valued and empowered, leading to higher retention rates and a more cohesive workforce.

Kaizen also contributes to better quality and customer satisfaction. Continuous improvement efforts focus on reducing defects, errors, and variability in processes, resulting in higher-quality products and services. By consistently meeting or exceeding customer expectations, organizations can build stronger relationships and enhance their reputation in the market. Furthermore, Kaizen's emphasis on regular review and feedback ensures that improvements are sustained and built upon, leading to long-term gains in quality and customer satisfaction. Overall, Kaizen is a powerful philosophy that drives sustainable growth and excellence in any organization.

S.W.O.T. ANALYSIS

SWOT Analysis is a strategic planning tool used to identify and assess the internal and external factors that can impact an organization's success. It stands for Strengths, Weaknesses, Opportunities, and Threats. Strengths and weaknesses are internal factors that the organization can control, such as resources, capabilities, and processes. Opportunities and threats are external factors, such as market trends, competitive dynamics, and regulatory changes. Conducting a SWOT Analysis helps organizations understand their strategic position and develop strategies to leverage strengths, mitigate weaknesses, capitalize on opportunities, and defend against threats.

The first step in a SWOT Analysis is to identify the organization's strengths. These are the attributes that give the organization an advantage over competitors, such as strong brand reputation, proprietary technology, skilled workforce, or robust financial health. Recognizing these strengths allows the organization to build on them and use them to achieve its strategic objectives. It also highlights areas where the organization can further invest to maintain its competitive edge.

Next, the organization assesses its weaknesses, which are areas where it lacks capabilities or resources compared to competitors. These could include factors like outdated technology, skills gaps, high operational costs, or poor customer satisfaction. Identifying weaknesses is crucial for understanding areas that require improvement. By addressing these weaknesses, the organization can reduce vulnerabilities and enhance overall performance and competitiveness.

The analysis then shifts to identifying external opportunities that the organization can exploit to its advantage. These might include emerging markets, technological advancements, favorable economic conditions, or changes in consumer behavior. Recognizing and acting on these opportunities can drive growth and innovation, helping the organization to expand its market share and increase profitability. Strategic planning based on identified opportunities ensures that the organization is proactive in leveraging external factors to achieve its goals.

Finally, the organization examines external threats that could negatively impact its performance. These could include economic downturns, regulatory changes, increased competition, or shifts in market demand.

Understanding these threats enables the organization to develop contingency plans and risk management strategies. By being aware of potential challenges, the organization can take preventive measures to mitigate risks and protect its interests. Overall, SWOT Analysis is an effective tool for strategic planning, providing a comprehensive view of the organization's internal and external environment and guiding informed decision-making.

The tools and techniques play a vital role in enhancing both product quality and operational efficiency. Beyond product improvement, these tools are adaptable for streamlining operations, whether in product development or service delivery. By identifying and eliminating waste, they help teams focus on tasks that truly matter. With tools like flowcharts, Pareto charts, and cause-and-effect diagrams, teams can break down processes into manageable chunks, organize them into a structured timeline, and target specific areas for improvement. This approach fosters clarity, ensuring all efforts align with strategic goals and timelines.

END NOTE

As I conclude "Behind The Fashionable Drapes", I reflect on the incredible journey of compiling these insights and tools. In the world of product development, countless techniques, tools, and strategies are constantly being innovated. While it's easy to get lost in this abundance, my aim here has been to present what I found most practical and adaptable—the approaches that, in my experience, are not only effective but also efficient to implement in real-world settings.

Each tool I've shared is more than a static solution; it's a flexible guide. Whether you choose to adopt, adapt, or reinvent these methods, remember that the most powerful resource you have is your own judgment. There's something wonderfully liberating about knowing that you can shape these techniques to meet the unique demands of your project. After all, it's not the tools themselves but the dedication behind them that sparks transformation.

Of course, commitment, teamwork, and an enduring passion are essential to navigating the complex paths in product development. With these, any challenge becomes a stepping stone to opportunity, a chance to craft something remarkable out of what initially seemed impossible.

This book is a product of my own learning journey, but it's also the beginning of a conversation. I would love to hear your thoughts, insights, and feedback. Reach out to me on LinkedIn at [Parvez Ahmed] (https://www.linkedin.com/in/parvezahmedp/), and on pparvez.ahmed@gmail.com, let's keep the dialogue going.

Here's to crafting solutions, seizing opportunities, and constantly evolving. Happy reading, and may your journey be as rewarding as mine has been.

ABOUT THE AUTHOR

Parvez Ahmed Peshimam stands as a titan in the realm of fashion corporates, wielding over three decades of expertise navigating its dynamic currents. From the corridors of senior management to the intricate operations that pulse at fashion's heart, his journey has been one of continual elevation and mastery. Armed with a Masters in Quality Management and certified as a Six Sigma Black Belt, Parvez embodies a commitment to excellence that shapes every endeavor.

Yet, beyond the boardrooms and strategic maneuvers, Parvez reveals another facet of his persona through the lyrical cadence of his writing. His literary odyssey commences with a debut collection of books, a testament to his creative verve and profound insights. This initial foray into the literary world signals the dawn of a promising career, with a multitude of projects poised to captivate readers in the near future.

Since settling in Dubai in 2003, Parvez has found both refuge and inspiration in the embrace of his cherished family. Alongside his beloved wife, Tanzim Parvez Peshimam, and their two enchanting daughters, Sarah and Safa, he discovers unwavering support and boundless motivation. They form the nucleus of his existence, infusing his pursuits with purpose and grounding his ambitions in the warmth of familial love.

With a narrative canvas richly textured by his vast experience, Parvez invites readers into a world where craftsmanship meets storytelling. His writings promise not just tales, but windows into realms illuminated by authenticity and profound understanding. Whether delving into the intricacies of fashion's inner workings or weaving narratives that resonate with universal truths, Parvez Ahmed Peshimam invites readers on a journey where each page unfolds with the allure of discovery and the wisdom of experience.